I0568617

ADVERSITY
FUELS
PURPOSE

ADVERSITY FUELS PURPOSE

CREATE A LIFE OF IMPACT AND SUCCESS

LANCE CIBIK

Adversity Fuels Purpose: *Create a Life of Impact and Success*

Copyright © 2025 by Lance Cibik

All rights reserved. No part of this book may be reproduced, distributed, or transmitted in any form or by any means, including photocopying, recording, or other electronic or mechanical methods, without the written permission from the publisher or author, except as permitted by US copyright law or in the case of brief quotations embodied in a book review.

Disclaimer: Although the publisher and the author have made every effort to ensure that the information in this book was correct at press time, and while this publication is designed to provide accurate information in regard to the subject matter covered, the publisher and the author assume no responsibility for errors, inaccuracies, omissions, or any other inconsistencies herein and hereby disclaim any liability to any party for any loss, damage, or disruption caused by errors or omissions, whether such errors or omissions result from negligence, accident, or any other cause.

Interior Layout and Design by Alice Briggs
Cover Design by Abigael Elliott
Editorial Team: Jeffrey Miller, Ginny Glass, Chloie Benton

ISBN:
979-8-89165-226-2 Paperback
979-8-89165-227-9 Hardback
979-8-89165-228-6 ebook

Published by:
Streamline Books
Kansas City, MO
streamlinebookspublishing.com

Streamline
BOOKS

DEDICATION

GOD, WITHOUT YOU, none of this would be possible. Thank you for being there despite life's adversities. I hope this book helps point others toward you.

To my wife and daughters. Thank you for your loving support throughout this journey. I couldn't have done it without all of you. You are my reason. Girl dads are the luckiest.

To my dad. Thank you for providing love and encouragement to me through all the ups and downs. You didn't give up. Love you, Pops.

To Land Hite. You continue to show up and model the behaviors to love and serve others just like Jesus. Thank you for doing life with me.

To Chad Hite. I miss you, but I promise to help carry the legacy that you left for so many of us.

To Tod Drury. Thank you for always believing in me, pushing me to higher levels, and for always being there no matter what. I am lucky.

To Will O'Rielly. For taking a shot on me and showing me what it means to be a true servant leader. Forever Boss.

To Greg and Bryce. Thank you for doing real life with me. 4—UncomMEN.

To Wojtek, Kenny, Dustin. My three brothers that have been there all along no matter what.

To Matt Doan. You came into my life at a critical juncture exactly when I needed you to show up. Forever grateful.

To the many friends and family members, you have been a part of this journey with me, every word, every page. You are a part of it all because you have done life with me. Thank you, and let's continue the ride together.

CONTENTS

Dedication v

Introduction ix

1   **Filling the Void** 1
     The Long Shadow of Loss 5
     Who Is the "Debbie" in Your Life? 7

2   **Be the Change** 11
     Living on My Own Terms 15
     Opening My Eyes to Others 18
     Hustling Hard 21
     Game-Time Mentality 23

3   **A Proving Ground** 27
     A Foundation of Empathy 30
     Reshaping Your Life and Future 32

4   **Climbing the Ladder** 35
     Three Core Principles of Success 38
     Stay Consistent 41
     The Skill of Communication 42
     From Success to Significance 43

5   Beyond the Ladder **47**
    Leaving the Corporate World 50
    Investing in Yourself 53
    Lessons Learned in the Corporate World. 56

6   The Accident. **61**
    Turning the Tide. 63
    Sharing My Story 65
    The Impact of Mentorship. 68
    Just Around the Corner. 70

7   Health, Wealth, and Self. **75**
    You Deserve a Better You 77
    Take Care of Your Health 78
    Take Care of Your Wealth 82
    Take Care of Your Self. 84

Conclusion. 87

About the Author. 91

INTRODUCTION

THE ODDS WERE stacked against me from the moment that I took my first breath.

I grew up in a family with parents living paycheck to paycheck, simply seeking to make ends meet. We enjoyed few privileges and lacked many resources or opportunities.

I don't blame my parents for this. As he was growing up, my dad's life was shaped by the absence of his own father. His dad and mom divorced when he was very young, leaving him to navigate life without a male role model. He never once heard his father say, "I love you." He never received a hug or even a pat on the back. The closest thing to affection he recalls was the occasional handshake during the rare moments when his father would briefly pop back into his life.

His mom worked tirelessly, holding down three jobs just to pay the bills. With her working long hours, my dad was often left alone. He spent his days mostly by himself in a house located in the woods of an apple orchard at the end of a long, isolated driveway. There were no neighbors nearby, and the road to his home wasn't even visible. So, my dad learned to fend for himself in many ways.

He started dating my mom when he was sixteen and she was fourteen. But as their relationship grew more serious, it created tension with his mom, especially as he approached his senior year of high school. His mom wanted him to focus less on his relationship and more on school, and she constantly pushed him to live out her version of what she wanted his future to be. But the control she tried to exert over him led to friction. Their relationship became so strained that, in the final weeks leading up to what should've been his high school graduation, the tension became unbearable.

That was a breaking point for my dad. He decided he was done and dropped out of high school. Although he later earned his GED, he now carried the challenge of having to make a living on his own without any real guidance or support. The truth is my father faced a lot of challenges and adversity. He even tried taking night classes in college, but life's pressures made it difficult to follow through.

I say all of this to give you a sense of how my life got started and what I was born into. None of this is meant as a slight against my dad or mom.

Still, that doesn't change the fact that the odds were stacked against me from the start. I wasn't born into the typical, idealized family situation: two college graduates with stable jobs, living in a nice, upscale neighborhood, sending their kids to private schools, money being set aside to help pay for future college education. Instead, I was born to a father who was in a challenging financial situation and a mother who had deep internal struggles.

But despite the challenges and circumstances I was born into, I have achieved a level of success in life and business that I didn't even know was possible. So perhaps my journey didn't start with a silver spoon in my mouth, living in a country club neighborhood, with a goldendoodle dog, and summer vacations to Disney or Caribbean resorts, but here's the thing (and I want you to hear this loud and clear): It doesn't matter! Even if the odds are stacked against you, you can still write your own story! You can decide to Be the Change for yourself and for your future family.

Now, you may have been born into better circumstances than me, where the odds were a bit more in your favor. Perhaps you grew up in a stable home with two parents who graduated high school or college, had steady jobs, and lived in an upscale neighborhood. Or maybe your circumstances were worse than mine. One of your parents spent time in prison, or drugs or alcohol had a grip on your household. Maybe you were born into crushing poverty or in a country where civil war raged around you and your family had to flee. Perhaps you experienced a health scare or diagnosis at birth or early in life.

YOU CAN STILL WRITE YOUR OWN STORY!

All of these struggles are real, but they don't have to define your future. Life may have dealt you a difficult hand, but that doesn't mean you're destined to lose. Where you start is just that—a starting point. What matters most is what you do from there and the choices you make moving forward. No matter what, you have the potential to achieve great things.

In this book, I'm going to share some very personal stories, but this book is not intended to be a memoir or an autobiography. I only want to use my own experiences to show you that the adversity we face doesn't have to hold us back. On the contrary, it can be the very thing that propels us forward. Your struggles, no matter how difficult, can become the fuel that drives you toward discovering your purpose and making a lasting impact on the world. As I've learned firsthand, success, whether in life or business, often comes from embracing hardships and using them as stepping stones toward growth.

It's inevitable: life throws obstacles in your path, sometimes from the moment you're born. But you're faced with a choice: Do you let those challenges define you, or do you push through them, adapt, and rise above? Now, of course, the definition of success is subjective, personal, and different for everyone, but the core message is the same for all of us: overcoming adversity can lead you to a deeper sense of purpose and fulfillment. Your adversity can become your advantage.

Maybe you will relate to some of my experiences. You might see your own life and struggles reflected somewhere in these pages and realize you're not alone. Indeed, if you're feeling stuck because of something in your past or you're facing a challenge today, I want you to know that I hear you, I see you, and I can relate to you. But more importantly, I want you to realize that you don't have to stay stuck.

You don't have to let the weight of your past or current struggles hold you down. Instead, you can take that energy and pivot. Use it as motivation to discover your purpose, to drive the impact you want to have in the world.

Along the way, I'm going to offer some principles, insights, and ideas that I hope will encourage you to think differently and to consider new approaches that can help you move forward. In the end, my goal is to help you turn adversity to your advantage and use all of your experiences to create a life filled with purpose, impact, and success.

ADVERSITY
FUELS
PURPOSE

CHAPTER 1

FILLING THE VOID

I WAS BORN TO parents who were high school sweethearts. They started dating when they were young, and after my mom, Debbie, graduated, they got married. She was just eighteen, barely a month out of high school, and there they were, stepping into marriage before either had really found their footing in life. They didn't have kids right away. In fact, they spent several years just trying to figure things out.

From what I understand, my dad wasn't eager to have children. His own childhood had been rough. His father, now separated from the family, never provided any love, affection, or guidance, so my dad essentially raised himself while his mom worked constantly. Understandably, the idea of becoming a father didn't appeal to him. He didn't have a role model to show him what it meant to be a dad, and in his mind, he didn't want to risk failing at something so important. Why would he want to bring a child into the world when his own experience of family life had been so fractured?

Despite this, my parents stayed together, but their relationship was fraught with turmoil. They sought counseling, and at some point during those sessions, the idea was floated that perhaps having a child might bring them closer together. And so, despite my father's reservations, they decided to try, and that's how I came into the picture.

Honestly, they weren't in a stable enough place in their marriage to have a child. They were just two young people trying to figure out life with a lot stacked against them. They were barely making ends meet financially, not getting along, and now they had a baby to take care of.

Despite the immense challenges I was born with, I was about to face another major obstacle in my life before I turned a year old.

Just four days before my first birthday, on May 2, 1981, my dad and I were asleep at home on a Saturday morning. My mom, however, had woken up early and left the house. She decided to drive her car to a nearby shopping center—a big, empty parking lot where most of the stores hadn't opened yet. She parked her car in a quiet corner near the dumpsters, away from the few other people who might have been out that early.

I often imagine what must have been going through her mind at that moment. She sat there alone, likely feeling overwhelmed by despair, anxiety, sadness, and hopelessness. The weight of her depression and fear must have been crushing, and she was wrestling with a decision that would ripple through so many lives—hers, mine, my dad's, and countless others.

You see, in that lonely moment, my mother decided to take her own life and commit suicide.

I think now about how much that decision changed everything for me and how fragile life is. My dad and I woke up to find three letters on the kitchen table. One was addressed to her parents, the second to my dad, and the third, the last one, was to me—her only son. Over the years, I've read those letters many times, and each time, I'm struck by her words. In her letter to my grandparents and to my dad, she asked them to always put me first and to take care of me in her absence. She talked about how difficult life was and how much she loved people, but they let her down, and she just couldn't go on anymore.

She explained in her letter to me that I was the best thing that had ever happened to her, but she still believed, somehow, that her decision was the right one. She told me, "Mommy loves you," but then she ultimately ended with, "Goodbye."

At the time, I was just days away from my first birthday. In fact, the very next day was supposed to be my birthday party. While friends and family were out buying decorations and presents to celebrate my first year of life, I had just lost my mother. I wasn't old enough to understand that the world had just become very different for me.

My mom was gone, and now it was just me and my dad. For my dad, the typical American Dream—a stable marriage, a child, the nice house with a white picket fence, the stability he was trying to create that he didn't have growing up—seemed further and further out of reach. He was now raising me alone, and he didn't have a model upbringing to draw from.

But that wasn't the end of the hardship—not by a long shot. On my mother's side of the family, the pain of her death ran so deep that many of them refused to accept that she had taken her own life. My mom was beautiful, kind, and in her late twenties. How could someone like her commit suicide? They couldn't believe it, and in their grief, they turned their suspicions upon my dad.

Despite there being no evidence, no signs of foul play, my grandmother, my aunt, and others on my mom's side were convinced my dad was not just my one remaining parent left to raise me, provide for me, love me, but instead, they would go on to suggest that my dad had murdered my mom. They pushed the police to investigate, trying to make a case that he was responsible. Even though the authorities found no criminal evidence, my dad passed a polygraph test, and the case was closed without a trial, they wouldn't let it go. They even filed a civil lawsuit, but that, too, was dismissed.

But their suspicions didn't die with the legal cases. As I grew up, my mom's family continued to find ways to plant seeds of doubt in my mind about my dad. Every visit with them felt like a subtle (or not-so-subtle) interrogation. I remember sitting at the kitchen table in my aunt's house, with her and my grandmother present. They pulled out this old cassette recorder and pressed the big red record button. And then they started asking me leading questions:

"Lance, you remember driving with your dad to that parking lot that morning, don't you?"

"You remember watching your dad take the gun and shoot your poor mom, don't you?"

They were trying to convince me, to make me recall something that never happened, as if I could remember details from four days before my first birthday. They were determined to make me question the man who was now my only parent, the one who was raising me.

As I grew older, the questioning continued, and it lingered in the back of my mind. There were moments when I wondered, Could they be right? Could my dad have been involved somehow? Their words stuck with me, and I found myself grappling with doubts about the man I was supposed to trust the most.

Sadly, the suspicions tore apart a family that had once been close. My dad, who had once been welcomed into their lives, became the enemy. The battle between my mom's side and my dad created a deep divide in my life, one that left me feeling conflicted and pulled in different directions. From my earliest memories, I was caught in the middle of this tension—on one side, my dad, who was raising me alone, and on the other side, family members who wanted me to believe he had taken my mom away from me. The effect on me was profound. I was too young to understand all the details, but I was old enough to feel the weight of what was happening.

The Long Shadow of Loss

As a young boy, a teenager, and even into early adulthood, I couldn't fully escape the doubts that lingered in the back of my mind. While I was 99 percent certain my dad didn't kill my mom, the persistent voices of my mom's side of the family—the people I was supposed to trust—wouldn't let me fully rest in that belief. My grandmother, my aunt, and my great-uncle continually tried to convince me otherwise, planting seeds of doubt that sometimes took root, even if just 1 percent.

Their insistence, despite the lack of evidence, played on my young, impressionable mind. It was like a small nagging thought I couldn't fully shake, even though my dad always offered to take another poly-graph test if I ever needed absolute proof. He would say, "If you have any doubts at all, just tell me when and where, and I'll do it." But I never took him up on it. I think deep down, I already knew the truth, but that sliver of doubt still gnawed at me, even when I didn't want it to.

But the real impact of my mother's death went far beyond the uncertainty about what had happened to her. What I struggled with most was trying to understand why she made the decision she did. If she loved me as much as she said in her letter, then how could she leave me just days before my first birthday, a time that should have been filled with celebration? There were moments of anger, confusion, and pain. I couldn't help but feel, at times, that maybe I wasn't important enough for her to stay. Those feelings of abandonment haunted me throughout my childhood and even into my adult years.

And then there was the simple fact of what I had lost—things I couldn't get back. Growing up without my mom meant missing out on her nurturing touch, her affection, the kind of love that only a mother can provide. I didn't have her to comfort me when I was sick, to be by my bedside and make everything feel better. She wasn't there to celebrate my wins at sporting events, to offer encouragement when things got tough. Watching other kids have their moms show up in these ways only deepened my sense of loss. It was like a constant reminder of what I didn't have, and it brought with it a sadness that stayed with me.

As I grew older, the long-term impact of losing my mom became even more apparent. There was a hole in my heart where my mother should have been—a presence I never really got to know but missed nonetheless. I found myself searching for that missing piece in different places and people. In many ways, I was looking for the love and nurturing that had been taken away too soon.

Over time, I realized that this void had created something else in me—a heightened sense of empathy and a deep desire to help others who might be feeling the same kind of loss or emptiness. I began to recognize the other "Debbies" in my life—people who were missing something, struggling, or just feeling out of place. And instead of being consumed by my own grief, I found a way to repurpose that energy into caring for them. It gave me a way to turn my pain into something positive.

I believe that the loss of my mother, while devastating, opened up a capacity for love and understanding that I may not have had otherwise. That drive to care, to support, to show up for people who need it, and to be more attuned to their hurts—that's how I've been able to move forward. It's how I've channeled my grief into something greater than myself.

As I developed a deeper sense of empathy, I started noticing how easy it is for people in difficult situations to be overlooked or forgotten. This awareness sparked a desire in me to step in where others might not.

For example, in high school, I found myself particularly drawn to students with physical and mental disabilities, kids who were often ignored or treated differently. While others might have looked past them, I was drawn to them and felt a special responsibility to show them care and attention. I began volunteering in their classrooms, and eventually, I started a program where other students could also spend time with them. The program allowed my peers to take time away from their regular classes to be with these students, offering friendship and kindness where it might have been lacking.

But it didn't stop there. I also sought out ways to help in my community, even in simple acts of kindness. Growing up as a young boy, I remember an elderly woman in my neighborhood who lived alone. She didn't have a husband, children, or anyone looking out for her. So, I stepped in. I would rake her leaves in the fall, mow her lawn in the summer, and help with household chores. These small acts of service weren't just about meeting her needs—they were my way of channeling the energy from the loss I had experienced into something meaningful.

That's when I realized that the void in my heart could be repurposed. Instead of letting the loss weigh me down, instead of feeling sorry for myself or dwelling on what I didn't have, I could use that energy to make a difference in others' lives. Every time I helped someone, every time I showed care or concern, it filled me with a sense of purpose. The more I served others, the more I found that the very act of helping others made me feel good. Their gratitude, their smiles, and their appreciation didn't just uplift them—it also helped to heal me.

In many ways, what I had lost in motherly affection, I gained in empathy for others. That empathy has become a driving force in my life. Even though I couldn't change my own past, I could change someone else's present.

Who Is the "Debbie" in Your Life?

So now I'll turn the question around to you. Who is the "Debbie" in your life? Who have you lost? Maybe it's a mother, a father, a spouse, a child, or a close friend. Where is the hole in your heart? Have you allowed the loss of that person to keep you stuck, sad, or buried deep in grief? Or, more importantly, have you figured out how to honor that person or repurpose the energy of that loss into something meaningful?

A couple of years ago, now as an adult with my own family, I was at home, looking out the front window, when I noticed my neighbor across the street struggling. Kathy is an older woman around the age my mom would have been if she were still alive. She's single, in her sixties, not married, and doesn't have children. That evening, I saw her trying to wrestle her large trash and recycling bins from the back of her house to the curb for collection the next morning.

As I watched, a thought struck me: If that was my mom struggling out there, what would I do? Would I just sit and watch, or would I go out there and help her? The answer was clear. I got up, walked out the front door, and offered her a helping hand. At that moment, I decided that Kathy would never have to haul her trash bins to the curb ever again.

It started simply enough. The next week, before Kathy even had a chance to move the bins, I did it for her. The week after that, I did it again. And soon, it became a weekly routine—taking the bins out and bringing them back after collection. I didn't say anything about it; I just did it, week after week, rain or shine.

Months went by, and one evening, as I was bringing the bins back, Kathy caught me as she was arriving home from work. She said, "Lance, you don't have to do this, but I can't tell you how much I appreciate it. There are days when work is stressful or the weather is awful, and the last thing I want to deal with is the trash. But you doing this for me, it just means so much."

I smiled and told her, "Kathy, I'm happy to help. But what you don't know is that there's more to this than just a simple act of kindness. If you have a moment, I'd like to explain."

I went on to tell Kathy about my mom. I shared how I lost her to suicide just four days before my first birthday. Growing up without her, I missed out on all the motherly nurturing and affection that most kids take for granted. Helping Kathy, I explained, was more than just taking out the trash. It was also my way of honoring my mom, of filling that void by caring for someone else. I couldn't be there for my mom, but I could be there for Kathy.

Kathy listened quietly, and when I finished, she nodded, tears in her eyes. She understood. It wasn't just about the trash—it was about transforming pain into love and loss into service. We shared a long embrace, and there were tears from both of us. It was a moment of deep connection, and that simple act of taking out her trash became so much more. It became the foundation for a beautiful bond between us.

I never had the chance to buy my mom a Mother's Day or Christmas gift. I never had the chance to hug her, kiss her, or tell her I loved her. And I never got to do something as simple as taking out the trash for her. But I can do it for Kathy.

What started as a simple gesture grew into an incredible relationship. Kathy began leaving containers of homemade soup on my doorstep. My family and I would come home from church, wondering what we were going to have for lunch, and there would be a big pot of soup waiting for us. Or we'd pull into the driveway after a long vacation, tired and hungry, only to find Kathy had made homemade enchiladas for us. She leaves thank-you cards, gift cards to my favorite restaurants, and even bags of my favorite coffee.

It has become a beautiful cycle of kindness. None of this was what I originally set out to do. I simply asked myself how I could take the loss of my mom and repurpose it into something meaningful. But in doing so, I eventually realized that while Kathy was benefiting, I was benefiting even more, both in how I felt and in the unexpected, tangible rewards.

Look, we all have losses in our lives, people who have left holes in our hearts. But instead of letting that loss keep us stuck, we can choose to repurpose it. We can take the pain and use it to make someone else's life just a little bit better. In doing so, we not only honor the memory of those we've lost, but we also heal a little bit ourselves.

So I'll ask it again: Who is the "Debbie" in your life? And more importantly, how can you repurpose that energy, that love, into something that brings light to someone else's life? Who is the "Kathy" waiting for you to show up? We all have the chance to take our pain, our losses, and turn them into something that benefits someone else. And often, when we do so, we discover that the impact on our own lives is far greater than we ever imagined.

Let me encourage you to make the decision today to use your adversity as fuel for your purpose. Look for ways to create an impact in someone else's life, and ultimately, as a result, they could show up as "soup" success in your own life. When you make that conscious choice, you'll find that it doesn't just benefit others. In fact, the greatest rewards often come back to you in ways you'd never expect.

The key is to delicately and intentionally shift your mindset from being a victim of your circumstances to becoming a creator of opportunity through those very challenges. You're not just overcoming adversity; you're transforming it into a powerful tool for growth and connection, where adversity can become an advantage. In doing so, you'll discover that life has a way of giving back tenfold, sometimes in ways that are as simple and profound as a pot of soup from a grateful neighbor.

CHAPTER 2

BE THE CHANGE

EARLY IN MY professional speaking journey, I had the opportunity to speak at a high school, and I remember thinking, How can I really connect with this group of high school athletes? It's not my usual audience, and I wanted my words to resonate with them on a level that felt genuine and relatable. So, I did a bit of research. I went on their school's website and saw that they had T-shirts made up for their athletic department. Each shirt had a slogan on it—simple phrases that embodied their school's spirit and mindset. One in particular stood out to me: Be the Change.

The idea of shifting your mindset, making the decision to take control of your own destiny, resonates with me very strongly, so I incorporated it into my talk that day. And, indeed, the kids leaned in and connected with the message.

To me, it's not just a catchy slogan. There came a time in my own life when I had to decide—and commit to myself—that the past would not define me, that the patterns of hardship and adversity would end with me, and that something new would begin. I was going to be the one to create a new chapter for myself and maybe for my family too.

The message was simple: It stops with me. And it starts with me.

You see, after my mom passed away, my dad remarried pretty quickly. Suddenly, I found myself in a new family with a stepmom who had three kids from a previous relationship, and, later, two more kids who were my half brothers. It was a chaotic blend of stepsiblings, half siblings, and me—the odd one out. I was the child from another mother, the "new kid on the block." I was different. I looked different, I talked different, and I performed differently—both in sports and in academics.

Being different made me an outlier in every way, and at times, it felt like a curse. There was a lot of misunderstanding and mistreatment. Honestly, we were all just navigating a messy, blended family situation. But the tension at home was palpable, and there were times when I would ask myself, How did I end up here? Why are these things happening to me?

Often, I felt singled out, treated unfairly, or blamed for things I didn't do. I remember one example so clearly: a lamp fell off a table, and the first reaction from everyone in the room was to point at me and say, "Lance did it!" even though I was nowhere near the table. It might seem like a small thing, but these kinds of incidents added up over time. And they had a way of reinforcing the idea that I was always the one at fault, always the outsider.

There were times when I was sent to bed early while everyone else got to stay up, watch a movie, eat popcorn, and laugh together. I'd lie in bed, smelling the popcorn and hearing their laughter echo through the walls, knowing I was missing out. I hadn't done anything wrong that day, but for whatever reason, I was the one punished. It was like living out a modern-day Cinderella story—except instead of being forced to clean, I was shut out from the simple joys of being part of the family.

There was no cartoonish wicked stepmother or cruel siblings plotting against me. Most of the time, it was more subtle—a quiet exclusion, an unspoken difference that set me apart. I didn't fit in. There were good moments too, of course. I don't want to imply that there was no love, no kindness. But there was also a lot of misunderstanding, and with it came a degree of mistreatment.

Things got bad enough that my dad and I would move out from time to time. Whenever I told him I'd been unfairly punished or mistreated, it would lead to an argument between him and my stepmom. The fights would escalate until one of us—usually my dad—decided it was time to go. I have vivid memories of the two of us packing up and finding a place to stay, sometimes for days, sometimes for weeks.

One winter, my dad and I ended up renting a mobile home. It was bitterly cold, and there was no central heat in the mobile home. The only way we could stay warm was by turning on the oven, opening the door, and letting it heat up the tiny kitchen. We prayed that the warmth would travel down the hallway into the cramped little bedroom we shared. I remember lying in that bed, the chill creeping in from the thin walls, thinking, This isn't how it's supposed to be.

Other times, we'd stay with a family from our church. They were kind enough to open their homes, but it was never ideal. I would sleep on the living room couch while my dad took the floor. There wasn't always an extra bedroom, and I could tell that, even though we were welcomed, we didn't quite belong there either. Eventually, some kind of fragile peace would be reached, and we would move back in with my stepfamily. But it never lasted.

This pattern of moving in and out went on throughout the years growing up in my stepfamily. And every time we left, it reinforced that feeling of not belonging—that I was somehow just passing through, never fully a part of this family, always on the edge of being pushed out. Now, I don't want to paint anyone in this situation as the villain. It was just the reality of being the "kid from another mother," the outsider trying to fit into a space that wasn't made for me.

It was rough, but then again, feeling like an outcast—an outlier—made me who I am today. It gave me grit, resilience, and the drive to prove myself, not just to others but to myself. It's why Be the Change means so much to me. Because I had to decide, against all odds, that I was going to become more than my circumstances. I wasn't going to let my past define me, and I certainly wasn't going to let it limit me.

Since then, I've met a lot of people who felt like the outcast, the outsider, the "kid from another mother." They felt out of place in their families, homes, communities, or schools. And it's not just a childhood thing. Even as adults, many still carry that sense of being different—whether it's because of their race, gender, religion, personality, or some other part of who they are. They've experienced one small injustice after another, and it feels like a slow erosion of spirit.

Even if you didn't grow up in a blended family, you've probably felt like an outcast at some point in your life. Maybe you were the only woman in a male-dominated workplace, or maybe you were the only person of color in an environment where everyone else looked different than you. Or maybe you just talk differently, dress differently, or hold different beliefs than the people in your workplace, family, or community.

If so, here's the thing: it's OK to be an outlier, and it's more than OK to be different. Indeed, sometimes, your uniqueness is the very thing that can make you stronger and more purposeful in life. You don't have to lose yourself to blend in with the people around you. On the contrary, you can appreciate the differences and lean into what makes you you.

During my early childhood, I was already deciding that I was going to Be the Change in academics and sports because those were the areas where I had control over how I showed up each day. I focused on getting straight A's and excelling in baseball, soccer, and basketball. These decisions gave me a sense of accomplishment and recognition that I didn't always receive at home. I knew that the choices I made and the effort I put in would eventually pay off as I got older.

Living on My Own Terms

I'd become a Christian as a young boy, but I started grappling with some heavy thoughts. As I was entering my early teenage years, I found myself wrestling with the idea that maybe this world really is an awful place. And if heaven is supposed to be so much better, why not try to get there sooner? I couldn't shake the thought that maybe my mom was right. Clearly, she had reached the point where she believed this world was so terrible that leaving it, even with all the ties and relationships she had—including me—was a better choice. And if she felt that way, maybe I should too.

I was thirteen, just sorting through my emotions and circumstances. I remember sitting on the floor of my bedroom one day, holding a wooden ruler with a metal edge. I was alone, and it felt like the walls were closing in on me like there was no escape. I thought, If I just keep going across my wrist long enough and hard enough, I'll eventually hit a vein. I'll bleed out slowly, silently. And then I can meet my mom again. Then I can finally get to heaven and leave all of this behind.

I started cutting, but I'm thankful I wasn't successful that afternoon. Somehow, for reasons I didn't fully understand at the time, I couldn't go through with it. But that moment was a turning point. It was the final straw for my dad. When he noticed the marks across my wrists, he realized that things between me and my stepfamily had gotten so bad that I was willing to end my life just to get away. He couldn't ignore it anymore. Despite pressure from the church to stay married and "keep the family together"—he made the decision to leave for good. He felt it was his duty to rescue me from that environment, and within weeks, he and my stepmom separated and, ultimately, divorced.

So that was it. That part of my story was finally over, and once we were gone, I put it behind me. After that, it was just my dad and me. My two half brothers and three stepsiblings stayed with their mom. For the first time in years, I felt a strange sense of freedom. With just my dad, I didn't feel the same oppression. I could breathe again, and I could focus on just being me.

We moved into a small apartment, just the two of us, and for a while, things were much better in my life. In many ways, I felt lighter. I didn't have to worry about walking on eggshells around my step-family, and I was free to find my own rhythm.

Unfortunately, that period of peace was short-lived. At the end of my junior year, my dad met someone new. He started dating a woman and wanted to move in with her. We had a long, difficult conversation about it, and he invited me to join them. But I was adamant—I didn't want to go. I didn't want to be thrust into another family dynamic with a woman I didn't know. I had already lost my mom to suicide and then been through the challenging dynamic of growing up in a stepfamily. I didn't want to go through all of that again.

I wanted it to remain just me and my dad for one more year until I graduated high school, but in the end, he still wanted to move in with her. He didn't force me to come along. He respected my decision to stay behind. But that meant I'd be living alone in my own apartment for my senior year of high school.

Now, I want to be clear: my dad didn't just leave me. It wasn't like he abandoned me to fend for myself. He offered me a choice, and I chose to stay. Plus, I had a small safety net—my mom's social security check came in every month, which helped cover rent and some of the basics. But I still had to supplement that income. I worked five days a week at a local grocery store and a restaurant as a server to pay for my car, insurance, cell phone, extra groceries, clothes—anything beyond the bare minimum. It wasn't easy, but for the first time, I felt like I had control over my own life.

Even now, looking back, I view that period with a sense of pride. I was just a kid—a teenager—learning to survive on my own. It was a crash course in self-reliance and independence. And as lonely as it sometimes felt, there was a kind of liberation in knowing that, for once, I wasn't beholden to anyone else's rules or expectations. I was just living life on my own terms, trying to make the best of the hand I'd been dealt.

That time shaped me in ways I'm still unpacking. It taught me resilience, grit, and a fierce determination to chart my own course. I learned that I could survive—even thrive—when the world felt like it was conspiring against me. And more than anything, it taught me that sometimes, being an outcast isn't a curse. Sometimes, it's the very thing that makes you strong enough to survive.

I was a teenager trying to piece together an adult life, and I had a choice to make. I had to decide what I was going to do with that life. I'd been born into a family that struggled to make ends meet, lost my mother four days before my first birthday, and survived a turbulent childhood bouncing between stepfamily dynamics. And now, I was standing on the edge of adulthood, with no one pushing me forward or pulling me back.

IT STOPS WITH ME. AND IT STARTS WITH ME.

Nobody in my family had ever gone to college. No one was in my face every day, pushing me to keep reaching higher. My world up until that point was small, marked by a series of obstacles that could've easily pinned me down and kept me there. But in that loneliness, in the quiet of my little apartment, I realized something: I could be the one to change the story. I could decide that whatever patterns, mistakes, and limitations had defined my family up to that point would stop with me. And anything better, anything more, would start with me.

It stops with me. And it starts with me.

So I made up my mind: I was going to Be the Change. I started looking around at the world outside my circumstances, at the kids in my high school who seemed to have it all together. They came from families of doctors, attorneys, and business owners. They wore name-brand clothes and drove nice cars. I'd see them glide through the hallways, smiling and confident, and think, Why can't that be me? I wanted what they had—the opportunities, the respect, the future that seemed so easily within their reach. But I knew I couldn't just want it; I had to take action and get it.

I started making changes. First, I focused on my grades. If I was going to have any chance of getting out of the cycle I'd been born into, I needed to prove I was more than just another kid from a broken family. I buckled down, spent late nights studying, and leaned on teachers who were willing to give me extra help. I transformed from an average, coasting student to the most improved—literally. By the time I was a senior, I received a small scholarship for being the most improved student from freshman to senior year (and graduating top of my class). It wasn't much, but it was proof that I could rise above.

Opening My Eyes to Others

By my senior year, I was no longer that lonely kid struggling in his stepfamily anymore. In a lot of ways, I had carved out a space for myself. I was a decent student, worked five nights a week, and was involved in athletics. I had friends and was considered relatively popular. From the outside looking in, you probably wouldn't have pegged me as someone who had ever felt like an outcast or an outlier. But that's the thing about appearances—they rarely tell the full story.

Despite how things might have looked, I never forgot what it felt like to be the kid who didn't belong. I knew what it was like to be misunderstood, to be judged without anyone really seeing who you were beneath the surface. Sure, I was a six-foot-two white guy with spiky hair who stayed in shape. I didn't have any physical or mental disabilities, but being in a family where I was the odd one out had affected me in ways I was still coming to terms with.

I carried those experiences with me everywhere, and they did more than just toughen me up—they opened my eyes to the struggle of others. I started to notice the students in the hallways who were truly on the outside, the ones who were more visibly outcasts than I ever was. The kids with Down syndrome or cerebral palsy. The ones in wheelchairs or those who made noises that others found "weird" or uncomfortable. I'd see people steer clear of them, crossing to the other side of the hallway, as if not knowing how to interact somehow justified ignoring them. And sometimes, the cruelty was more direct. I'd see students snicker or whisper, and it hit me in a way I couldn't fully describe.

Despite my own life being worlds apart from theirs, I felt a connection. I knew a little something about what it was like to be different, to be the one others whispered about, the one no one quite knew how to handle. I had been there too. Maybe not with physical or mental challenges, but certainly with a heart full of hurt and a mind wrestling with feelings of isolation.

So, I decided to do something about it. I went to my teachers and asked if I could spend an hour each day with the special education class. At first, it was just me. I'd sit with these students, eat lunch with them, read to them, or just talk. I wanted to show them that someone saw them, that they weren't invisible, that they were more than just their disabilities. I felt a sense of purpose when I was with them, a fulfillment that no amount of high school accolades or social status could ever give me. I could see it in their smiles, in the way they lit up when I walked in the door. They needed to know they were valued. They needed to know that they were people, just like everyone else.

Before long, other students started to notice. They'd ask me, "Hey, Lance, what are you doing in there?" and I'd tell them. A few of them started joining me. And then a few more. Eventually, a small group of us were getting permission to skip out of certain classes so we could spend time in that special education room. We'd sit in circles with the students, read books, play games, and eat lunch together. Something small was happening—something that didn't show up in yearbooks or trophies—but it was real. A connection was forming.

And it didn't stop there. I started volunteering at Special Olympics events, cheering them on as they raced or competed. One of the greatest honors I had was at the high school graduation ceremony when I got to push one of my friends from that class down the aisle in his wheelchair. Another moment I'll never forget was walking hand-in-hand with a girl who had Down syndrome, helping her proudly make her way across the stage to receive her diploma.

I'm not sharing this to give myself a pat on the back, and I'm not looking for recognition. The point is that out of my own experience of being an outcast, I found a well of empathy that I never would've tapped into otherwise. I realized that the very thing I hated about my past—feeling isolated and unseen—was actually a gift waiting to be unwrapped. It gave me the ability to see others who were overlooked, to connect with them in a way I couldn't have if I'd never been through it myself.

It taught me something powerful: being an outlier isn't a weakness. It's a strength. It's a perspective. And it's a tool you can use to make the world a little bit better, a little more inclusive. Feeling different, feeling outside the norm, gives you a unique vantage point, one that allows you to see people others ignore, to empathize in a way that's genuine and meaningful. If you can take that pain and flip it, if you can use it to fuel acts of kindness and connection, then you can turn it into a force that changes not just your life but the lives of those around you. Your adversity becomes an advantage.

If you've been an outcast, if you've been made to feel less-than, it's not the end of the story. There's power in that feeling. There's purpose in it. You can choose to let it make you bitter, or you can let it break you open and make you more compassionate, more understanding, more human.

So, yes, those years were hard, but they shaped me into someone I'm proud to be. They made me more aware of the impact we can have when we choose to give back, when we choose to see people for who they really are instead of what sets them apart. And that's what I want anyone who feels like an outcast to know: you have something unique to offer. The very things that make you feel different can be what make you the most powerful—if you choose to use them for good.

Because at the end of the day, being on the outside gives you a different kind of strength. It gives you the ability to see, to feel, and to connect in ways others might not. And if you can channel that, you can build bridges where there were once walls. You can turn isolation into inclusion. You can be the change you wish someone had been for you. That's what I learned then. And that's what I try to live every day.

Hustling Hard

Everyone has moments lying in bed at night, thinking about all the things they wish they could do. But most people just keep thinking and never do anything about it. I didn't want to be one of those people. So while others were staying up all night playing video games, mindlessly scrolling through social media, or hanging out with the wrong crowd, I worked to build my future.

I got a job as a host at a local restaurant, then eventually moved up to being a waiter. I worked five nights a week to help cover the bills. I'd watch people my age breeze through their carefree teenage years, partying and goofing off, and I'd be at the restaurant, closing down every night, scrubbing tables and sweeping floors until midnight.

I wasn't just working—I was hustling. I wanted to go further than the people around me, so I put in the extra reps, the extra time. While my classmates were just getting by, I was hitting the books harder, meeting with teachers for extra study sessions, and working shifts no one else wanted. I chose to work Sundays from lunch through dinner, pulling double shifts while others clocked out early to spend time with friends or significant others. I saw every extra hour as another small step forward.

It wasn't just about the grind; it was about proving to myself that I could rise above where I started. That's what I mean when I talk about hustling hard. It's not just showing up and doing what's expected; it's pushing yourself to do what others won't. And that work ethic became my edge. It allowed me to stand out, not just in school but in life. If someone was working hard, I wanted to work harder. If someone was studying, I wanted to study longer. I started looking around at the people to my left and right, in front of me and behind me, and thinking, How can I outwork every single one of them? How can I gain an edge? Stand out?

And that's how I developed a game-time mentality. I approached every challenge with a mindset of, I'm ready; I'm prepared. Whether it was a test, a shift at work, or a new opportunity, I wanted to be ready to execute at the highest level. Anyone, anywhere, anytime—I was willing to take on whatever came my way. I wanted to be prepared for anything because I knew I'd put in the time when no one else was watching.

And so, by the time I walked across the stage at high school graduation, I wasn't just another statistic—a kid from a broken home who didn't have a chance. I was ready for whatever came next. I had already faced the worst life could throw at me, and I'd survived. I had risen up and changed my path. I wasn't the kid I had been when I started high school. I was something else entirely—someone who knew what it meant to fight for every inch, to hustle when everyone else quit, and to play the long game when the odds were stacked against me.

I still remember walking somewhere in the rain one afternoon, as a cold drizzle soaked through my clothes, and thinking to myself, This is nothing. I'm going to keep walking, keep moving forward, because I've faced worse and come out the other side. I was ready for anything, and that's a power no one could take away from me.

Game-Time Mentality

A "game-time mentality" means putting in the work when no one else is looking, staying ready for any challenge that might come your way. It's a mindset built on the belief that if you put in the sweat, the practice, and the extra reps, then you will be prepared for anything. Whether it's game day, test day, or job interview day—you're ready. I looked at life the way an athlete looks at the field on a Sunday morning: Your field, my field, let's go. Let's execute. I am ready for any opponent—anyone, anywhere, anytime.

That mentality carried me through the last stretch of high school and right into college. All of that hard work turned out to be worth it. I graduated at the top of my high school class and earned a single, precious opportunity: the chance to go to college. No one else in my family had done it. Alongside the small scholarship, I was able to scrape together enough in federal grants and student loans to make it happen.

And just like high school, college wasn't some idealized experience for me. There were no frat parties, no lazy Saturdays, no spring break beach trips. I never joined a fraternity because I knew it would be a distraction. I skipped out on parties, avoided the wrong crowds, and stayed away from anything that could pull me off track. I couldn't afford to lose focus because I didn't have time for any of that. I was methodical—almost military in my focus. I mapped out every semester, every class, every credit hour. My goal was simple: get straight A's and set myself up for a career that would take me somewhere. Somewhere far away from the small apartment I was barely managing to pay for with my restaurant wages. I still worked five nights a week and all day Sunday just to keep a roof over my head and make ends meet.

While other students were out enjoying the freedom of being away from home, I was stacking textbooks at a corner table, fitting in study time between shifts. I'd start my day at the crack of dawn, go to classes, squeeze in homework wherever I could, and then head to the restaurant in the evening, often working until midnight or later. It wasn't glamorous, but I knew that's what it took. If I wanted a future different from the past I'd left behind, then every second counted.

College was a grind. It wasn't the "best four years of my life" that people often talk about, but it was the most important. Because for the first time, I felt like I wasn't being held back. I wasn't being limited or suppressed by my circumstances. I was truly free. And with that freedom came a sense of responsibility. If I was going to make something of myself, it had to be now. I couldn't blame anyone else. I couldn't point to my past. There were no excuses.

By the time I graduated, I had a 3.8 GPA, earned a spot on the chancellor's list, and walked away with a degree in business and finance. It felt like I was standing at the summit of a mountain after years of climbing—bloodied and bruised but standing.

Looking back, I realize the lessons I learned during that time were worth more than any degree or academic award. I learned that success is built on thousands of tiny choices—decisions made in the quiet, mundane moments when no one is watching. It's deciding to get out of bed when you don't want to. It's choosing to go to work when everyone else is hanging out. It's hitting the books harder, staying an extra hour, saying no to distractions, and never allowing yourself to get too comfortable.

In order to Be the Change, it wasn't just going to be a one-time decision; it was going to be a commitment I had to make over and over again. Every day. Every hour. Every time I clocked into work or opened a textbook, instead of picking up the TV remote. It was a decision to keep pushing when quitting would've been so much easier. People would often ask if I had seen a TV show or movie or remembered the lyrics to a song, and my answer was always the same, "I don't have time for that. I am on a mission."

And more than anything, I learned that if you want something bad enough, you can create your own opportunities. I couldn't control where I'd started, but I could control how I responded. And when I made up my mind to rise up, hustle hard, and keep my head in the game, doors started to open. Opportunities I never thought possible began to appear.

CHAPTER 3

A PROVING GROUND

I SEE MY COLLEGE years for what they were—a proving ground. A place where I discovered what I was truly made of. The truth is, we all have those defining moments—whether it's in a classroom, a workplace, or at a kitchen table late at night. It's not about where you start; it's about the mindset you build, the actions you take, and how hard you're willing to hustle when no one's watching.

YOU CAN CHOOSE TO RISE UP.

That's what carried me through those years. That's what turned a kid living alone in a tiny apartment into a college graduate with a business degree and a vision for something more. So hear me clearly:

No matter your circumstances, no matter where you are right now, you can choose to rise up, to take action. You can choose to hustle. And with that game-time mentality, you can get yourself ready for whatever life throws your way. The circumstances you're born into, the struggles you face, and the injustices you've endured—none of those things have to define you. It's easy to let them hold you back. It's easy to let them become excuses, to let them become the reason you give up or never try in the first place. But it doesn't have to be that way. When life throws something at you that you don't deserve, you get to choose your response.

In the midst of my struggles, I discovered that the pain, frustration, or rejection I was dealing with could become an energy source if I looked at it the right way. It wasn't about ignoring it or pretending the pain didn't exist. It was about redirecting it—taking what should have torn me down and using it to build myself up.

Now, that's not always an easy thing to do, especially when you're young, alone, and feeling like life has dealt you a pretty bad hand. But I knew that if I didn't choose that path, I'd be stuck forever, trapped by the very things I wanted to escape.

Look, we all have our own struggles. For me, it was my family, my loneliness, the feeling of not belonging. For someone else, it might be something totally different. Maybe they grew up with a health condition that made life harder. Maybe they were the kid who always felt too tall, too short, too heavy, or too thin. We all have something. Something that makes us feel like we're on the outside looking in. No matter what it is for you—even if you've been dealt a hand that feels unfair—you can still choose how you respond.

I know a lot of people, even adults, who are still wrestling with things that happened in their childhoods. They're stuck in it, whether they know it or not. Maybe it's something they've never talked about, something that's still festering deep down. Maybe it's anger. Maybe it's shame. Maybe it's a belief that they're not good enough. And that pain ends up showing up in other areas of their life—in how they treat people, how they approach work, how they think about themselves.

So whether you're a high school student reading this who's just starting to figure out who you are or a middle-aged adult who's never fully let go of something that happened decades ago, I want you to understand one thing: you have the ability to turn all that pain, fear, and rejection into something powerful.

Every one of us has the opportunity to take whatever "different" thing we've been carrying and make it our fuel. But first, we have to face it. We have to look it in the eye, acknowledge it for what it is, and decide that it's not going to control us anymore. For me, it started with embracing the fact that I was an outsider, that I didn't have the same support or resources as other kids my age. Once I owned that, I could see a path forward.

You don't have to be defined by the things you can't control.

Whether it's your upbringing, your appearance, your financial situation, or any of the other circumstances that feel like roadblocks, you have the power to decide what you do with them. You have the power to write the next chapter.

I see this time and time again when I speak to people. I've talked to kids who feel overwhelmed

YOU DON'T HAVE TO BE DEFINED BY THE THINGS YOU CAN'T CONTROL.

by their home life, and I've talked to adults who are still haunted by experiences from decades ago—stuff that they've never even admitted to anyone. It's like a quiet weight they've carried for so long that they don't even realize it's there. And it affects everything: how they think about success, how they relate to others, and how they see themselves. But I always tell them, "It doesn't have to stay that way."

You can redirect that energy. You can turn it into something else—something that propels you forward instead of holding you down. That's what I did. I took all that pain and isolation and frustration and funneled it into my grades, my work, my ambition to be something more. I focused on what I could control—my effort, my response, my mindset. I found ways to surround myself with people who represented where I wanted to go, not where I'd been.

And over time, those little choices added up. They took me from a kid living alone, struggling to make it through high school, to a college graduate with a clear vision for my future. If I could do that—if I could change my trajectory—then anyone can.

Success in life isn't about having the right start; it's about choosing the right response. No matter where you are, no matter what you're carrying, you can decide to be the change by shifting your mindset, to rise up and take action, to hustle hard by putting in the extra reps, and to get into a game-time mentality to battle anyone, anywhere, anytime. Because, at the end of the day, it's not about being the best. It's about becoming the best version of yourself despite everything that's tried to hold you back.

A Foundation of Empathy

People often ask me, "What's your secret to success?" I have to laugh a little whenever I hear that question because, honestly, there's no grand strategy or master plan. If anything, my so-called secret sauce has been a really simple one: I just show up and care about people. I've done that since I was a teenager waiting tables, all through college, and into my career and relationships. It's just who I am. I've always tried to take a genuine interest in others, and it's opened more doors and created more opportunities than I ever could've imagined. I love what I heard a pastor once say: a way to be humbler and to keep the focus off yourself is to stay constantly curious, always asking people questions about themselves—who are they, what do they need, how can you help them.

It's not something I've ever done for applause or recognition. In fact, I'm not even sure I realized how rare it was until I started working in corporate America. That's when it hit me—most people aren't wired that way. They're so focused on their own ambitions, their own success, their own goals that they often miss what's right in front of them: other people. People who are aching to be seen, to be heard, to be valued. If you can see them, truly see them, it's like a switch flips. Everything changes. You connect, and that connection creates a bond that's more powerful than any sales pitch or business strategy.

It sounds simple, but it's rare. I remember a moment that drove this home for me. A senior leader—a person I ended up reporting to for a short period of time—decided they had it out for me. They lived in another city, so we were remote colleagues, at best, and they did not know me well. We'd hardly interacted at all. But for some reason, they began trying to create a false narrative about my character that went against the reputation I had built for years. They went so far as to say that I needed empathy coaching to better understand the people I served in the situations they were in.

Ironically, that was probably the last thing I needed, as thousands of team members and clients that I had worked with during my career of twenty years could attest to, while this particular leader may be the one that was actually lacking in empathy. I learned a hard lesson through that experience. Sometimes, people in positions of power will use that power against you to make themselves look better, and they might even project their own insecurities or weaknesses onto you in the process. This senior leader didn't really know me; they didn't even want to know me. They only wanted to strengthen their own position and power, and they didn't mind seeking to destroy my reputation to do it.

The truth is, people—whether they're colleagues, customers, friends, or family—don't just want to be sold to or managed. They want to be seen. They want to be known. They want to feel valued. When you lead with empathy, when you show up with an authentic desire to connect, you're not just changing their experience—you're changing your own life too.

I believe that's why empathy and genuine care are such recurring themes in my life. They've been the foundation of every success I've had, whether in business or relationships. The ability to see beyond

IMPACT IS THE ULTIMATE DEFINITION OF SUCCESS.

the surface and recognize the human being standing in front of you is where real impact starts. And for me, impact is the ultimate definition of success. It's not about money or titles or accolades; it's about making a difference. It's about leaving a mark on someone's life, even if it's in a small way.

Growing up and feeling like an outsider is why I can't help but notice when someone else is on the margins, when they're struggling or hurting. It's why I started volunteering with kids who had special needs back in high school, why I made time to walk the hallways with students who most people avoided, and why I dedicated hours every week to helping out in the special education classroom. I wasn't doing it for recognition—I was doing it because I knew what it was like to be overlooked, and I wanted to make sure someone else didn't have to feel that way.

I've carried that focus on empathy into every part of my life. And I think it's important for anyone reading this to understand that empathy isn't some soft skill that makes you weak or vulnerable. Empathy is a strength. It's a tool that, when used right, can create incredible impact. It's not just about being nice; it's about truly understanding what others are feeling and using that understanding to build trust, to create loyalty, and to make someone's day a little bit better.

Reshaping Your Life and Future

Rising up and taking action is perhaps just a more actionable way of saying, "Be the change." This idea has become the moral compass guiding me through the chaos of my life. When everything around me felt turbulent—losing my mom, moving between families, and struggling to find where I belonged—I realized I couldn't control the world, but I could change how I showed up in it. By being the change I wanted to see, I could reshape my life and my future.

In high school, this mindset became my fuel. I wanted better grades, a stronger work ethic, and a healthier body. So I chose to embody the discipline and resilience I admired. I studied harder, worked extra shifts at the restaurant, and hit the gym five days a week. It wasn't about waiting for circumstances to improve. It was about creating the improvement myself.

This approach carried me through college and beyond. Every semester, I set a vision for myself: straight A's. But it wasn't just about grades, it was about proving to myself that I could rise to the challenge. I worked five nights a week, stayed focused, and lived out the change I wanted in my life.

Today, in business and life, I hold that same belief. Instead of seeking control, I choose impact. I say no to distractions, whether it's a toxic relationship, a fleeting idea, or a low-priority project because staying true to my principles and purpose is what drives real change. The ripple effect is undeniable.

EMPATHY IS A STRENGTH.

When you live with purpose and act with intention, you not only transform yourself but also inspire others to do the same.

But here's the thing: being the change isn't just about results. It's about connection. It's about leading with empathy, caring deeply for others, and lifting people up along the way. When you commit to growth, not just for yourself but for everyone around you, you create something meaningful. Success becomes more than just what you accomplish. It's who you become and the legacy you leave in the lives you touch.

What change do you want to see in your life or business? How can you simplify, focus, and show up consistently to create that change, not just for yourself but for the people you lead and love? The answer lies within you. Be the change. Start today.

CHAPTER 4

CLIMBING THE LADDER

WHEN I LOOK back on my work history, I realize that my first real training ground wasn't in some prestigious internship or corporate setting—it was, as I mentioned in the last chapter, a bustling restaurant, waiting tables night after night during high school and college. It may not seem like the most obvious stepping stone to a successful business career, but for me, that job was more than just a way to make ends meet. It was where I learned some of the most valuable lessons about people, hustle, and the power of controlling my own outcomes.

I chose to work as a waiter for a couple of reasons. First and foremost, it was a commission-based role. That meant my paycheck was directly tied to how well I performed. If I showed up with energy, put in the extra effort, and really focused on giving my customers a great experience, I'd walk away with more money in my pocket than the guy working the next table over.

It was a game of effort and reward, and that motivated me. Unlike an hourly job where I'd make the same wage regardless of how much I poured into each shift, waiting tables meant I could push myself to be better, to move faster, and to deliver better service. In short, I could control my own success.

That job gave me a front-row seat to understanding my "controlling the controllables" philosophy. I learned early on that I couldn't control every factor—maybe a customer would be in a bad mood, or maybe the kitchen would run out of a popular dish. But I could control how I responded. I could focus on my attitude, my work ethic, the speed of my service, and the experience I delivered to every person who sat at one of my tables. I leaned into that idea and realized that if I did everything in my power to give my best effort, more often than not, the results would follow.

And I loved the environment. Being a waiter wasn't about punching a time clock and zoning out for eight hours. It was a fast-paced, high-energy job that let me be on my feet, moving from table to table, interacting with people, and trying to find ways to make their night just a little better. I'd race back to the kitchen to grab a pitcher of sweet tea or bring out an order before the guest even had to ask. But more than the physical hustle, what I loved most was the personal interaction.

Each night, I'd challenge myself to really connect with my customers. I'd ask them about their day, their work, their families. I'd ask what brought them into the restaurant that evening. Was it a special occasion? A date night? Just a quick dinner on the way home? I'd listen to their stories, remember their names, and try to find small ways to make their experience memorable. It came naturally to me, this curiosity about people, this genuine interest in getting to know them, and it made my shifts more than just work. They were opportunities to build connections.

What I didn't realize then was how those hours of waiting tables were setting the stage for the next chapter of my professional life. When I finally graduated with my business and finance degrees and stepped into the corporate world, I found myself using those same skills that had made me a successful waiter. I just traded in my apron for a business suit.

I spent twenty years as an investment consultant and coach to financial advisors. My territory ranged from two to six states, and my role was to meet with advisors one-on-one, in small groups, and in large training events. I'd travel from city to city, booking appointments, leading workshops, and standing in front of rooms filled with seasoned professionals, sharing strategies and coaching them on how to build their practices.

But at the heart of it, I was still doing what I'd done at that restaurant. I was asking questions, listening intently, and trying to connect on a deeper level. Sure, the setting was different, and the stakes were higher, but the core approach was the same. I'd sit across from an advisor and start with simple, genuine questions: "Tell me what's working well for you." "What are you struggling with right now?" "What would success look like for you in the next year?"

It might sound basic, but you'd be surprised how rare it is to find people in corporate settings who ask those kinds of questions and mean it. Most are more interested in getting through their checklist of tasks or pushing their own agenda. But when you take the time to really listen and let people know that you see them as more than just a number, it changes everything. They open up. They trust you. And that's where the real work—the meaningful, impactful work—begins.

If I had any success in corporate America, it started with being curious about people and caring enough to dig beneath the surface. I think a lot of people underestimate just how powerful it is to show genuine interest in someone else. So often, we're caught up in our own goals and ambitions, our own to-do lists, that we forget to slow down and really see the person in front of us.

That's why I say that, in a lot of ways, I'm still just a waiter at heart. I may have gone on to get a business degree, earned my spot in corporate America, and climbed the ranks, but at the end of the day, I'm just a guy who believes in serving others. I believe in being attentive, in anticipating needs, and in treating everyone I meet—whether it's a diner at a restaurant or a CEO in a boardroom—with the same level of respect and genuine care.

It's a simple approach, but it has served me well. Because people don't just want solutions or strategies—they want to know that they matter. And if you can show them that, if you can take that extra step to truly understand and connect, that's where real success happens. Not just in business, but in life.

SHOW PEOPLE THAT THEY MATTER.

So, whether I was racing around a restaurant floor trying to keep up with orders or navigating high-stakes meetings with financial advisors, the guiding principle was always the same: show people that they matter. Everything else, whether it's sales, success, or relationships, falls into place from there.

Three Core Principles of Success

Ultimately, success isn't some mysterious formula. It's not about flashy strategies, fancy degrees, or even being the smartest person in the room. I believe it comes down to a few simple, almost mundane principles that most people overlook. I didn't stumble upon them all at once; I pieced them together slowly over years of experience, starting from my time waiting tables all the way through my corporate career as a consultant, coach, and leader. The way I see it, it all boils down to three core principles:

1. Show up with genuine curiosity,
2. Do what you say you're going to do,
3. Control your controllables.

The first principle comes straight out of my time as a restaurant server. I was showing up curious. That might sound almost too simple to matter, but you'd be surprised how rare it actually is. Early in my career, I realized that being genuinely curious about people made all the difference. It's one thing to show up to a meeting, nod along, and get through the agenda. But it's another thing entirely to sit down with someone, look them in the eye, and actually listen—really listen—to who they are, what they're dealing with, and what success looks like to them.

It's not about pushing your own agenda; it's about letting them know that you see them. Most people don't do that. They're too caught up in their own narratives, their own goals, to take the time to understand someone else's perspective. But when you're sincerely curious, you build trust. And trust is the foundation of any lasting success.

That second principle—do what you say you're going to do—hit me hard. I remember early on, when I was just starting to get a foothold in the corporate world, sitting down with a client who'd been in the business for decades. He was blunt, a straight shooter—the kind of guy who'd seen it all. I was fresh-faced and full of energy, armed with all these ideas I thought would blow him away. But after I laid out my recommendations, he leaned back in his chair and said, "Look, Lance, I see people like you all the time. You come in with great ideas, say you're going to do three things, and then I never hear from you again." He paused and looked me dead in the eye. "If you want to be different—if you want to be successful—just do what you say you're going to do."

It sounds almost ridiculously straightforward, but it's rare. People love to make promises, to talk a good game, but follow-through is where so many fall short. That client's words stayed with me, and I decided then and there that I would be different. I would always follow through. If I told someone I'd send them a report by Friday, they'd have it in their inbox before noon. If I said I'd circle back with more information, I'd make sure they didn't have to chase me down to get it.

Doing what I said I'd do wasn't just about being reliable—it was another way of showing people they mattered. It was about proving that their time and their trust weren't taken for granted.

Most people don't do this consistently. They get caught up in their own lives, their own distractions, and before they know it, that promise they made slips through the cracks. But if you can just show up, be curious, and follow through every single time, you're already setting yourself apart from 90 percent of the people out there.

The third principle is one we've already touched on, one that has been a guiding force for me: controlling your controllables. Life, business, and the world in general are full of distractions and things outside our control. The news is chaotic, inboxes fill up faster than we can empty them, and people don't always do what they're supposed to do. It's easy to get caught up in it all, to waste time worrying or complaining about what isn't going right. But I learned early on that focusing on what you can't control is just spinning your wheels. Instead, I put all my energy into controlling what I could.

This mindset was something I clung to during my early years of struggling to make a name for myself. I couldn't control where I was born, how much money I had, or what other people thought of me, so I leaned into what I could control—my effort, my discipline, and my focus. I couldn't change what others did, but I could control how I showed up. If I was going to work five nights a week as a waiter, then I was going to be the best darn waiter in that place. If I was setting out to achieve straight A's in college, then I was going to out-study, out-prepare, and out-focus anyone else.

That same mentality carried into my corporate career. I didn't get sucked into unproductive meetings just to look busy. I didn't waste hours sending emails that didn't move the needle. I stayed focused on what really mattered—the core responsibilities and results that I was hired to deliver.

Stay Consistent

I always tell people, "Keep it simple. Stay consistent. Achieve results." Complexity breeds confusion. The more complicated a plan or strategy, the easier it is to get off track, to make excuses, to find reasons why something didn't work. But if you can strip things down to their essence—figure out what really matters, focus on doing those things well, and then do them over and over with relentless consistency—that's how you achieve results.

This mindset works in business, and it works in life. Whether it's fitness, nutrition, or career success, the idea is the same: keep things simple and stay consistent. I often use the analogy of health and fitness. If you want to get in shape, you don't need a complicated diet plan or an expensive gym membership. You just need to keep it simple: eat whole, clean foods, exercise regularly, and stay consistent. Five days a week, week after week. The results will come, but only if you avoid the distractions and stay true to the basics.

I've watched countless companies and teams get lost in layers of bureaucracy, overwhelmed by systems and processes that add complexity but not value. They overthink, overplan, and overcomplicate until they can't see the forest for the trees. But the most successful businesses, the ones that thrive year after year, are the ones that keep things simple. They focus on what really matters. They identify their key priorities and stick to them with discipline and focus.

That's what I've tried to do throughout my career: show up curious, do what I say I'm going to do, and control my controllables. It's not flashy, but it works. And in a world that often values complexity for complexity's sake, sticking to those simple principles can be your greatest advantage. Because while others are running in circles, caught up in the noise and chaos, you're quietly, steadily moving forward—step by step, day by day—achieving results that speak for themselves.

The Skill of Communication

When I think about the skills that have made the biggest difference in my career, there's one that stands out time and time again—communication. It's a skill that goes hand-in-hand with everything else we've just talked about.

Communication is something I've focused on and refined year after year because I've learned that it's the key to everything. It doesn't matter how great your product is, how cutting-edge your service, or how visionary your company's strategy—if you can't communicate your ideas clearly and connect with the people on the other side of the table, it's all meaningless.

I've come to believe that the real differentiator, the thing that sets you apart in a crowded field, is the ability to communicate effectively and present your ideas in a compelling way. It's not just about the words themselves but about making sure that what you say is received, understood, and remembered.

And communication is more than talking—it's about truly connecting. One of the lessons I've held onto, and one that's carried me through every promotion, every client interaction, and every leadership role, is understanding that people want to be seen. They want to be heard. Whether it's a client sitting across the table or a team member in a one-on-one meeting, people want to feel valued. They want to know that they matter, that their opinions count, and that someone is genuinely interested in what they have to say.

This is a basic truth of human nature. Even the most selfless among us, at the core, care about ourselves. We're wired that way—we have to be. We think about our own needs first: Am I fed? Am I safe? Am I valued? And that doesn't change just because we walk into a business setting. It's something I remind myself of constantly, whether I'm speaking to a team of financial advisors, working with a direct report, or talking to someone in my family. When I show up to a conversation, I try to set aside my own agenda and focus on what matters most to them. What are they really concerned about? What are they working toward? What makes them feel valued?

If you can stay focused on that, if you can put yourself in a position where you're leading with empathy and understanding, then everything changes. It shifts the dynamic from "What do I want out of this?" to "How can I help this person get what they need?" And that's where real value lies—whether you're in sales, leadership, or just trying to be a good friend or spouse. That's the heart of it.

From Success to Significance

Looking back over my twenty-year career in financial services and corporate America—climbing the ladder from assistant vice president to senior vice president, winning awards, and accumulating titles—it's easy to get lost in the surface-level achievements. I worked my way up through the ranks, traveling constantly as I built my career, one meeting, one promotion, and one territory at a time. Yes, I wore the custom-tailored suits, drove the BMW, stayed at the Ritz-Carlton, and had the fancy dinners at high-end steakhouses. I lived in a nice neighborhood, took luxury vacations, and achieved the kind of success that looks shiny from the outside. But somewhere along the way, I started asking myself a question: Now what?

When I was at the top of my game professionally, I hit a wall. My net worth was growing, my titles were stacking up, and I had all the outward signs of success, but there was a hollow feeling that I couldn't fill. Was this really it? Was this what I had worked so hard for? Just a never-ending pursuit of the next title, the next paycheck, the next shiny thing? It felt like being stuck on a treadmill, running faster and faster but not really getting anywhere that mattered. I started to wonder if I was losing myself in the process—sacrificing my health, my relationships, my family time all for the next rung on the corporate ladder.

And I wasn't alone in feeling that way. Over the years, I've talked to countless colleagues and friends who have found themselves in the same spot—plugged into a system, chasing the next achievement, the next rank, the next milestone. But what happens when you finally reach that goal? You think it'll feel like crossing a finish line, but instead, you're just staring at the next race, already lined up, already waiting for you to start running again.

For me, the real wake-up call came during the COVID-19 pandemic. The world slowed down—business trips were canceled, the back-to-back meetings on my calendar thinned out, and suddenly, I was spending more time at home than I had in years. Instead of rushing through airports and living out of hotels, I was at the dinner table with my family. I was waking up in my own bed instead of in some sterile room miles away. And that forced me to take a hard look at my life. I started to ask myself what success really meant to me. Was it just the titles, the income, the lifestyle? Or was there something deeper I needed to be pursuing?

That's when I began to shift my focus from success to significance. I realized that it wasn't enough to just be successful in the traditional sense. I didn't want to climb the ladder for the sake of climbing. I wanted to do work that mattered, to make an impact that went beyond a job title or a paycheck. I wanted my life to mean something more than just numbers on a balance sheet or a list of accomplishments.

That shift wasn't easy. It required me to redefine what success looked like for me. I had to let go of the constant chase for external validation and turn inward to figure out what I truly valued. So I began asking myself tough questions: Am I making a difference? Am I showing up for the people who matter most to me? Am I living in alignment with who I want to be?

What I came to realize is that significance starts with connection. It starts with empathy, with listening, with being present for the people in your life—whether that's your family, your team, or your clients. It's not about how much you achieve but about how you achieve it. It's about showing up with intention, making the people around you feel seen and heard, and leaving a positive mark on every life you touch.

So when I think about my career and all the lessons I've learned, it comes down to this: Success is about what you achieve, but significance is about what you leave behind. I've done the success thing. I've climbed the ladder. But now, I'm more focused on what I can build that will last, what I can contribute that will outlive me. Because at the end of the day, titles and accolades are temporary. But the impact you make—the lives you touch, the people you uplift, the difference you make—that's the legacy that endures. That's the path I'm on now, and I can tell you this: it's a far more rewarding journey.

SUCCESS IS ABOUT WHAT YOU ACHIEVE, BUT SIGNIFICANCE IS ABOUT WHAT YOU LEAVE BEHIND.

CHAPTER 5

BEYOND THE LADDER

THOUGH THE ISOLATION of the pandemic inspired me to reconsider what success meant to me, there were two specific moments in my life that finally got me to reconsider the never-ending climbing of the corporate ladder. The first one happened when I lived in Seattle. I had been promoted into a high-status role, managing a large territory that spanned four states, and I was on the rise in corporate America. There was a certain prestige attached to the work—the kind that came with traveling, high-level meetings, and a constant stream of attaboys and applause on stage at company events. I should've felt like I was on top of the world. But the truth was, I felt incredibly far from everything that really mattered to me.

Back home on the East Coast, in Charlotte, North Carolina, were my dad and brothers, and just a little farther up in Cleveland, Ohio, were my grandparents, aunts, and uncles. My grandmothers were well into their nineties, and I'd grown up visiting them during the summers, sitting on their porches, and listening to their stories. I remember thinking about all the time I was missing—birthdays, holidays, the simple joy of sitting around a dinner table together. I'd hear about family get-togethers I couldn't attend because I was 3,000 miles away, jetting off to another business meeting, and it hit me: Is this really worth it?

One evening, as I sat alone in my hotel room, the rain pattering against the window, I felt the emptiness of it all. I had achieved so much on paper—titles, promotions, money—but I wasn't there for the people who mattered most. My two grandmothers, each approaching the end of their lives, were spending their final years without me around. I thought about how, one day, I'd be getting that inevitable call telling me they were gone. And I'd be left with nothing but regret for the time I'd traded for a job that felt so important at the moment but seemed utterly insignificant compared to the people I loved.

That realization was a turning point. I knew I had to make a change, even though it would be disruptive to my career. I'd only been in the Seattle role for a short time, and it had come with a promotion and a bigger territory. Moving back to the East Coast meant I'd have to step down, take a hit to my status, and start over in a new position. But I kept asking myself, Ten years from now, what will I regret more—taking a step back in my career, or missing my family's last days? The answer was clear.

So, I started looking for opportunities that would bring me back home. I found one in Charlotte, took the leap, and never looked back. In the end, I was able to spend more time with my family—something I could never have replaced with any title or salary. That decision, as tough as it was at the moment, taught me that success isn't just about climbing higher and higher. Sometimes it's about knowing when to step back, to refocus on what really matters before it's too late.

The second moment utterly changed my view of corporate America, and it was a hard pill to swallow. It's an incident I mentioned earlier. I had worked my way up at a large company, with a long tenure and a solid reputation. My performance reviews were consistently high, my relationships with clients and colleagues were strong, and I had racked up years of awards and recognition. I felt secure. There was a senior leader who came into the picture, and almost immediately, I could tell something was off.

This person, for reasons I still don't fully understand, decided to make me a target. Without warning, they started questioning my competence, painting a narrative that I wasn't suitable for my role, and even claiming that most of my peers didn't trust me or value my guidance. I was blindsided. After years of building a reputation and consistently delivering results, I was suddenly being portrayed as the problem. And the worst part? None of it was true.

I couldn't comprehend how someone who barely knew me could walk in and, in a matter of weeks, start tearing down everything I'd built. I kept telling myself that the work I'd done—as well as the people who knew me and my track record—would speak for itself. But this leader seemed intent on making things difficult for me, creating a false narrative to suit their own agenda, and using their position to undermine my credibility. I went from feeling respected and valued to doubting my own abilities.

That experience was a harsh lesson. It opened my eyes to the darker side of corporate culture—the politics, the power plays, and the unsettling truth that not everyone above you has your best interests at heart. I had always thought that if you did your job well, treated people right, and delivered results, you'd be safe. But I learned the hard way that that isn't always the case. Sometimes, it doesn't matter how good you are or how solid your reputation is—if the wrong person decides you're a threat or simply doesn't like you, they can make your life miserable.

It made me realize just how vulnerable we all are when we work for someone else. I'd always bought into the idea that if I just worked hard and played by the rules, I'd keep moving forward. But suddenly, I saw how fragile my success was, how quickly it could be taken away. It wasn't about my performance; it was about politics, power, and personal agendas.

That experience changed me. I began to see that tying my identity and self-worth to a job title or a company's approval was a dangerous game. Because, at the end of the day, some corporate leaders can be fickle. They'll cheer you one minute, and the next, they'll tear you down because it suits someone else's goals.

So, I started to shift my focus. I realized I needed to create a foundation that couldn't be so easily shaken by someone else's opinion or agenda. I began thinking less about climbing the corporate ladder and more about how I could build something meaningful, something no one could take away.

It was a tough lesson, but one I'm grateful for now. Because it pushed me to find my own path, to focus on what really mattered, and to ensure that no matter what happened in the corporate world, I would never again let someone else have the power to define my worth.

Leaving the Corporate World

The moment I finally stepped away from corporate America wasn't as dramatic as you might imagine. There wasn't a grand exit or a definitive final day where I walked out of a glass office building with my box of personal items, shaking hands and saying farewell to colleagues. In fact, part of me still hesitates to even say I've left the corporate world entirely. For all I know, six months from now, someone might offer me a role I can't turn down, and I'd be back in it. But at the time of writing this, I'm not in that world—and for now, that feels right.

The truth is, the decision to leave corporate America wasn't a single leap. It was more of a slow unlearning of everything I'd been conditioned to believe about career, success, and identity. For years, I had plugged myself into the system, taking job after job, building my resume, always aiming for the next rung on the ladder. That's what you're supposed to do, right? You get in, you do your job well, and then you figure out how to stand out enough to get promoted—to earn more, gain more influence, and keep climbing. I never questioned it. I just thought that's what everyone did.

But now, it felt like I'd been stuck in a box—a very successful, well-compensated box, but a box nonetheless. But what if there's more? What if climbing the corporate ladder isn't the only way to live a fulfilling life? What if all the skills I'd honed in corporate America—the same ones that had gotten me those promotions and praise—could be put to use in ways that didn't require reporting to a manager or adhering to someone else's vision?

That mindset shift didn't happen overnight. In fact, I didn't even see it coming until it was right in front of me. It started when I began working with a business coach, someone who challenged me to really look at what I loved doing, what energized me, and what felt like my "zone of genius"—the kind of work that feels effortless, almost enjoyable, even when it's tough. My coach asked me to think about the compliments I'd received over the years. What did people always seem to come to me for? What made me light up in meetings, even in the most stressful situations?

I started to notice a pattern. Throughout my career, whether I was leading a team or working directly with clients, what I loved most was connecting with people—helping them see things in a new way, guiding them to perform at a higher level, and motivating them to push past their perceived limits. I thrived in that role, whether it was in a one-on-one setting or in front of a packed room. When I started looking back on the feedback I'd received over the years, one thing stood out: people valued my ability to coach, to mentor, and to inspire. It was the common thread running through all my successes.

So, with the encouragement of my coach, I began to wonder: What if I could get paid to do this on my own? What if I didn't need a corporate title to be significant? What if I could take that same skill set that had brought me success in the corporate world and turn it into something of my own?

That's where the idea of becoming a professional speaker and performance coach started to take shape. I began to see that the very things I'd been pouring into my corporate roles could be used outside of that structure. I realized that there were people—entrepreneurs, business owners, and other professionals—who would value my insights, my experience, and my ability to help them achieve their goals, just as I had done for countless colleagues and clients in my corporate life.

But leaving corporate wasn't just a logistical move; it was an emotional one too. There's a certain identity that comes with working in corporate America, especially when you've been there for as long as I had. It's not just a job; it's your status, your sense of security, your validation. I'd spent years attaching my self-worth to my title and the accolades I received. I wasn't just Lance Cibik—I was a senior vice president with a polished resume, a track record of success, and a steady stream of performance awards. Stepping away meant redefining who I was without all of that.

When you've built your entire professional life within the structure of a corporation—fighting for the next promotion, hitting your performance targets, and gaining respect from your peers—the thought of leaving can feel like stepping into a void. There's no more corporate ladder to climb, no more titles to chase. Just you and whatever you decide to build next.

But that's exactly where I found the freedom I'd been searching for. I started to realize that my significance didn't come from my title or my paycheck. It came from the impact I made on the people around me. Whether I was a senior vice president or an independent consultant, that wouldn't change. I still had the same skills, the same passion, the same ability to make a difference. The only thing that shifted was how I chose to channel it.

When I stepped out of the corporate world, I made a conscious decision: I wasn't leaving behind my drive, my ambition, or my desire to succeed. I was simply choosing to define success on my own terms. Instead of chasing another title, I started to focus on significance—on building something that would allow me to help others, connect with people in a meaningful way, and create a lasting impact.

Investing in Yourself

There's a practical reason why I'm sharing this story. It's not because I think you will find my career story so very fascinating. Rather, there's something I hope to help you discover about yourself.

If you find yourself in the corporate world, feeling like you've hit a ceiling or plateaued, there are more options than just fighting for the next promotion or jumping ship to another company. You have a unique skill set, a set of strengths that can be leveraged in ways you might not have considered yet. Maybe it's starting your own business, maybe it's consulting, or maybe it's just finding a side project that brings you joy and fulfillment. Whatever it is, the important thing is to realize that your value isn't tied to a company's org chart or your spot on a performance review.

Your significance is something you carry with you, no matter where you go or what role you're in. Stepping away from corporate America wasn't the end for me—it was the beginning of a journey to redefine success and to build something that feels true to who I am. And while I don't know what the future holds, I know this: I'm no longer just chasing a title. I'm building a life of purpose and meaning, and that's a pursuit worth every risk I've taken along the way.

If I could go back and talk to my younger self, the one just starting out, full of ambition and energy, standing at the bottom of the corporate ladder and staring up at what looked like an endless climb,

I'd tell him to lean into every opportunity that corporate America provides—but to do it with his eyes wide open.

Corporate America is an incredible training ground. It's a place where you can learn, grow, build your skill set, and expand your network. There are mentors to meet, strategies to master, and experiences that will shape you in ways you can't yet imagine. The company will invest in your professional development—sending you to trainings, paying for certifications, and offering you a steady paycheck while you build your resume. So take advantage of every bit of it. But don't let it define you. While your job can be an amazing vehicle for growth, it should never become the source of your identity or the place where you seek your self-worth.

That's where a lot of people, myself included, get stuck. You step into this environment and start getting good at what you do. You get recognized, promoted, and the validation feels intoxicating. It starts to become part of who you are. And before you know it, your title is more than a job description—it's your identity. Your success is tied to your last performance review, and your self-worth rises and falls with every quarterly target. It's a dangerous game to play because the reality is, no matter how loyal you are, no matter how hard you work, the company's priorities can change in an instant.

I've seen it happen too many times. Layoffs come out of nowhere, restructuring happens, or a new manager steps in, and suddenly, despite years of hard work, you find yourself on the outside looking in. It's not personal; it's business. That's why, if I could, I'd tell my younger self—and anyone just starting out—not to get too comfortable. Don't let your job be the only thing that defines your value.

BUILD YOUR SAFETY NET.

Instead, I'd say this: build your safety net. Grow your network and treat every person you meet as a valuable connection. Get to know people, not just in terms of what they can do for you, but on a genuine, human level.

Gather their contact information and take notes on who they are, where they're from, and what they're passionate about. Add them to your LinkedIn, keep up with them, and make yourself memorable. Because your relationships will carry you far beyond your current job or role. They are what will help open doors when you least expect it and when you most need it.

Another thing I wish I'd understood earlier is the importance of investing in yourself—not just in the ways your company offers, but on your own dime. Too many people think that their college degree is enough and that the company they work for will handle the rest. But the truth is, you should never rely solely on your employer to shape your future. Take it upon yourself to seek out courses, certifications, and professional development opportunities that make you stand out. Learn how to communicate better, present your ideas more powerfully, and sharpen your soft skills. These are the traits that will make you resilient and adaptable no matter what industry changes or corporate shake-ups come your way.

Investing in yourself isn't just about building a better resume—it's about building a stronger you. It's about making yourself the kind of person who can thrive no matter where you land. Because the corporate landscape can be fickle. One day, you're a rising star. The next day, you're dealing with an unexpected layoff. But if you've invested in your skills, your education, and your relationships, then you're never truly vulnerable. You're ready for whatever comes next.

And that's why I'd also encourage anyone starting out to think beyond just climbing the ladder. Don't get me wrong—the ladder can be worth climbing. There's value in proving yourself, in striving for promotions, in gaining leadership experience. But keep your options open. Don't lock yourself into one path without considering others. Maybe one day, you'll want to take those skills and start your own business, pivot into consulting, or take on a side hustle that brings in additional income. Maybe you'll want to shift industries or go freelance. It's about creating options for yourself so that your success is never dependent on a single job or a single employer.

This is what I'd call career insurance. It's making sure that, no matter what happens in the corporate world, you're not left scrambling. It's having a side project or business that you've been nurturing, a robust network that you can lean on, and a diverse set of skills that makes you valuable beyond just your current role. That way, if the day comes when corporate America no longer serves you—or you no longer want to serve it—you're ready. You're prepared. You're not starting from zero.

So climb the ladder. Learn everything you can. Build relationships. Get promoted if that's what you want. But always keep in mind that your identity is so much bigger than any title or company could ever define. Find ways to nurture your own interests and passions outside of work. Take time to build something for yourself.

A career isn't just about titles or paychecks. It's about building a life that's fulfilling, that's balanced, and that's yours. So yes, embrace the opportunities that corporate America gives you, but remember: you're not just an employee. You're a whole person with talents, dreams, and potential that go far beyond the confines of any one job.

If you can do that, you'll be building something far more valuable than a career—you'll be building a future that's truly your own.

Lessons Learned in the Corporate World

Honestly, so much of those twenty years in the corporate world are a blur—a constant cycle of meetings, travel, and deadlines. However, some of the things I learned during those years have stayed with me. The simplicity of my approach stands out. I kept things basic, never overcomplicating my strategy or getting lost in the noise. I focused on what I could control: setting appointments, building relationships, and showing up every single day with consistency and purpose. That was my formula, my secret sauce.

Every day, I made it a point to do the little things right. I'd walk into meetings with one goal—to connect. I'd sit across from someone, whether it was a new client or an old colleague, and make it my mission to truly get to know them. I'd ask about their life, their struggles, and their goals. What kept them up at night? What were they working toward? And I did it not because I was trying to check a box or follow some sales script but because I genuinely wanted to understand the person sitting in front of me. I knew if I did that—if I listened, if I made them feel seen—trust would follow.

That was my edge in what I call the sea of sameness. In corporate America, everyone can start to look the same. We all wear the same suits, use the same jargon, and boast the same credentials. So, what was going to make me different? How could I stand out when, on paper, my job title and qualifications were nearly identical to the person next to me? I decided early on that the answer wasn't in being louder, flashier, or more aggressive. It was in being genuine. It was in showing up, day after day, being curious, being reliable, and following through on every promise I made.

That's how I built my reputation, one interaction at a time. I stayed relentlessly focused on the basics: getting in front of people, listening to their needs, following up, and delivering on what I said I would do. And I did it over and over and over again. There's a power in consistency that people underestimate. When you do the right things, even small things, repeatedly, they add up. It's like compounding interest in a bank account—small, steady deposits of trust and reliability that grow into something bigger over time.

While others were content to coast, I was pushing forward. When some of my peers would leave work early to go out drinking or lose themselves in binge-watching Netflix, I'd be studying. I wasn't doing it because I had to but because I knew that every hour I spent investing in my skills was an hour that put me ahead. I'd hit the books for another certification, tackle another professional designation, or read up on industry trends. I knew that in order to differentiate myself, I had to be better than just good—I had to be exceptional. And that didn't happen by accident. It happened by making deliberate choices every single day.

But when I stand here today, looking back at it all, the things that stand out aren't the performance awards or the sales targets I crushed. It's not the bonus checks I received or the high-end dinners I could afford. Sure, those moments felt great at the time, and I appreciated what they bought me—the vacations, the nice car, the satisfaction of knowing my hard work had paid off. But none of those things are what linger in my memory.

What I cherish most are the relationships. The people I met, the bonds I built, and the shared moments of laughter and struggle—that's what stays with me. I don't miss the numbers or the accolades; I miss the conversations. I miss the coffee meetings where we'd talk about our kids, the late-night strategy sessions where we'd problem-solve until we finally cracked it, the road trips where I'd ride shotgun with a colleague and we'd swap stories about life, work, and everything in between.

It's those human connections that made the grind worthwhile. All the metrics and measurements, all the quotas and goals, they were just byproducts of focusing on people. I didn't see clients or coworkers as transactions. I saw them as people with lives and dreams and families, just like me. And that's what I'm proudest of—that through it all, I never lost sight of what really mattered. I made sure every interaction counted, that I brought my full self to the table every time. Because, in the end, business isn't about numbers or titles—it's about people.

There's a phrase that I've held onto over the years: "Keep it simple. Stay consistent. Achieve results." It's how I approached my career, but it's also how I approached building relationships. I didn't need a complicated strategy or a groundbreaking technique. I just needed to show up, stay true to who I was, and do the work—day after day, week after week, year after year. And by keeping it simple, by staying consistent, the results took care of themselves.

That's why, when I look back on everything I accomplished, what stands out isn't the awards or promotions. It's the people who'd call me for advice long after I'd moved on to a new role. It's the handwritten notes of thanks I'd receive. It's the moments when someone would pull me aside and say, "You really made a difference for me." That's the stuff that lasts. That's the stuff that matters.

REAL SUCCESS ISN'T MEASURED BY WHAT YOU ACHIEVE—IT'S MEASURED BY THE LIVES YOU TOUCH ALONG THE WAY.

So, if there's one thing I'd pass on to anyone looking to set themselves apart in that sea of sameness, it's this: Focus on people, not titles. Focus on consistency, not shortcuts. And never forget that real success isn't measured by what you achieve—it's measured by the lives you touch along the way.

CHAPTER 6

THE ACCIDENT

THROUGHOUT MY TWENTIES and thirties, I was entrenched in the high-stakes world of corporate America, working within financial services. Looking back, I see how much of that time was spent either running from my past or relentlessly chasing success. I pursued titles, accolades, awards, certifications, and designations as if they defined me.

My worth felt inseparable from my title, my income, my ability to save and invest. The proof of my "success" was everywhere: my 401(k) statement, the kind of apartment I lived in, the car I drove, the clothes I bought, and the restaurants and bars I frequented. Each external sign of achievement reinforced that I was winning in life. I had proven that I could climb the ladder from assistant vice president to vice president and eventually senior vice president.

In many ways, my life looked successful—both on paper and from the outside. But even as I ticked off one success after another, questions began bubbling up. What would marriage mean for me, someone who came from a family marked by divorce? How would I navigate my Christian faith, which had been a foundation in my childhood but had taken a backseat in the fast-paced world I was now immersed in? I was living a life full of accolades and achievements, but it didn't feel as fulfilling as I thought it would. Beneath the surface, there were things I hadn't faced.

I had no idea the nightmare that lay just around the corner.

One night in my early thirties, my friends invited me out to a local bar. It was a Saturday night, and I thought, Sure, why not? I figured I'd just have one beer, stay cautious about driving, and, if need be, leave my car and take a taxi or Uber home. As I made my way to meet them, I passed Ed's Tavern, another local bar that sits near a busy intersection in Charlotte. It was not my destination; I just happened to be driving by. Ed's Tavern was packed. There was a Duke versus North Carolina basketball game being played on TVs inside of Ed's Tavern, and the energy was high. People were inside, people were outside, all mingling and drinking. My senses heightened as I saw the crowd standing outside in the front of Ed's Tavern, not knowing that inside the bar, two men were in the middle of an altercation.

One highly intoxicated man hit on another man's girlfriend. The other man confronted him, and angry words were exchanged. The situation escalated, eventually spilling out of the bar. The intoxicated man, in his impaired state, stumbled out onto the street just as my car was passing. I didn't see him until it was too late.

My two-seater BMW, a low-to-the-ground sports car, struck him, and I felt every moment of the impact, the sickening crunch as he went under the tires. It was as if I had driven over a large log, a jarring sensation that I still feel today. I came to a stop, trying to process what had just happened. Had I really hit someone? Where had he come from? Was there something I could've done to avoid this? I replayed it all in my mind in those split seconds—had I been drinking too much? Was I speeding?

It was surreal, as if he had dropped from the sky right in front of me, giving me no time to react. Glancing in my rearview mirror, I saw people gathering around his motionless form. Panic set in. Did he have friends there? Would they be angry, possibly violent? All these thoughts raced through my mind, but I managed to pull myself together enough to call 911.

The medics and police arrived, and the man was pronounced dead. I was taken down to the station for further questioning, given a breathalyzer, and spent hours there, answering questions until the early morning. The days that followed were some of the hardest of my life. I had already been grappling with deeper questions about faith, life, and my values, but now, I had to process the reality that my actions—though unintended—had resulted in a man's death. It didn't matter that I couldn't have prevented it. I was the one driving the car that struck him.

For weeks, I could barely bring myself to get behind the wheel again. This incident forced me to confront everything I had been avoiding, and I had no choice but to face the questions I had buried under my so-called success. It was the beginning of a new reckoning with myself, one that would challenge my definition of success, my values, and, ultimately, my purpose in life.

Turning the Tide

In the wake of the accident, I found myself questioning everything, especially my faith. Why would God let something like this happen? How was I supposed to process the guilt and grief and find a way to move forward?

What I didn't know at the time was that someone from my past had read about the accident. An ex-colleague of mine named Land Hite, a man I'd only worked with briefly years earlier, saw my story in the paper. He also saw news of the man who had been accused of second-degree murder for allegedly pushing the victim into the street just before my car hit him. Charges against the man never held, but Land knew both of us—the man accused and me. Though he and I weren't friends and had barely spoken during the year we worked together, he felt a deep sadness reading about my situation. As he later told me, he felt an undeniable nudge from the Holy Spirit to reach out to me.

One day, I received a handwritten note in the mail. Land had taken the time to write, saying he'd read about the accident, was deeply sorry, and wanted me to know that God loved me. He included his phone number with a simple offer: if I ever wanted to talk or grab a cup of coffee, he was here. In that dark season, he was the only person who had taken the time to write me a personal handwritten note.

That one gesture turned the tide. One call turned into many, one cup of coffee into countless breakfasts, lunches, and conversations. Land became a steady presence in my life exactly when I needed it. He didn't just meet up with me—he poured into me. He cared, listened, and offered a compassionate ear as I grappled with questions about life, business, faith, and purpose. His support helped me untangle feelings and thoughts I hadn't dared to face. And I couldn't help but wonder, why did he care so much? We weren't close, we didn't share an age group (Land is twenty years older than me), and our lives hadn't intersected meaningfully before. Yet, there he was, week after week, month after month, year after year, consistently showing up.

Because of Land, I found myself on a path I hadn't envisioned. With his guidance, I developed the courage to make choices that eventually led me to meet my wife, start a family, and experience fatherhood with our two daughters. A few years later, after I had grown through that season of my life, Land asked me if I would spend some time with his son Chad, who was struggling with addiction and mental health issues. Chad was about ten years younger than me, and he was facing his own challenges and searching for answers.

My initial meetings with Chad were like mentor and mentee, but quickly, we connected in a deeper, more authentic way. Chad was open and raw about his struggles. He didn't hold back, sharing everything he was dealing with—the good, the bad, and the messy. His honesty was a powerful invitation, and it allowed me to be real in return. The more he opened up, the more I did. Our time together evolved from mentorship to friendship, a connection forged in vulnerability.

Over time, Chad made his way through recovery and found a renewed purpose. He decided to go back to college to specialize in drug and alcohol addiction recovery, hoping to help others who were walking the path he'd walked himself. He even started a podcast called The Rabbit Hole, where he shared his story and hosted guests who had overcome their own battles. Each episode became a source of hope and encouragement for people struggling with addictions, adversity, or personal crises. Chad had found a way to turn his pain into a lifeline for others by using his past struggles as a platform for healing.

Looking back, I can see how this journey unfolded with purpose. What began with one small, handwritten note from a near stranger in Land Hite became a thread that wove through my life, helped me find my own strength, and eventually gave me the chance to pass it on to someone else in his son, Chad Hite.

Sharing My Story

Chad's journey led him to start speaking at schools and sharing his story to warn students about the impact their choices could have. He wanted them to understand that their decisions could lead to hardship, but he also offered hope—if they found themselves in trouble, there was a path back. Chad's life became an example of what could happen when you lose your way and, just as importantly, what's possible if you find the courage to reclaim your life.

He eventually began working at Charlotte Rescue Mission, a non-profit that provides a free, four-month program for men battling addiction. There, Chad dedicated two or three nights a week to supporting these men, guiding them through the struggles he knew so well. He was in a unique position to help them—he understood their pain, their doubts, and the deep battle with addiction. In many ways, he was showing up for his past self.

Then, one day, Chad turned to me and said, "Lance, you've got a story. You've faced your own adversity. You've overcome challenges—why don't you come on my podcast and share it?" I resisted at first. I was completely uninterested in speaking about my life on a platform where, theoretically, anyone in the world could hear it. But Chad was persistent, and eventually, I agreed to join him on The Rabbit Hole. I shared my story, hoping it would encourage someone out there dealing with their own hardships.

After the podcast, Chad kept pushing. "Why don't you start speaking in schools, Lance?" He believed in the power of sharing our stories with others, and he knew from his own experience that honesty and vulnerability could resonate deeply. I resisted again, reluctant to open up in such a public way. But Chad led by example, and when the opportunity came to share my story with a men's group at my church, I finally agreed.

With Land and Chad sitting in the front row, I spoke, and their presence gave me the courage to keep going. That talk led to more opportunities, and before I knew it, I was speaking at schools, delivering messages of hope to students facing difficult family situations or financial hardships. I wanted them to believe, like I had come to, that no matter where they started, they could find success and meaning in their lives.

Around that time, I joined a local men's networking group that hosted weekly speakers. One day, I saw Chad was scheduled to speak there, and I noticed an open slot the week before. I thought, Well, if Chad is doing it, I can do it too. So I signed up, gave my talk, and the following week, Chad took the stage. Standing there, introducing Chad to the audience and watching Land beam with pride from the front row, I felt a sense of purpose I hadn't anticipated.

Chad's encouragement had sparked something in me, and it was only growing in intensity. I decided to lean into professional speaking. I began taking professional speaking courses, launched a website, created a demo reel, and started marketing myself as a speaker. I wanted to carry the message that no matter the challenges, there is always hope on the other side of adversity—a message I'd watched Chad bring to life in his own way.

But then, just a few months after we'd both spoken at that networking event, tragedy struck. One Sunday night in 2024, Chad was on his overnight shift at Charlotte Rescue Mission. After all the men had gone to sleep, he went to his own room for the night, just like any other shift. But the next morning, he didn't wake up. Chad passed away in his sleep that night at thirty-three years old, and with his passing, the world lost a powerful voice for hope and redemption.

As I think back on those moments, it's hard not to feel the weight of what he left behind. Chad's life—and his loss—continues to push me forward to carry the message that he so bravely shared. His courage and compassion were a gift that changed my life, and now, I'm committed to honoring his legacy by showing up, sharing, and giving others a glimpse of hope when they need it most. Chad had used his past adversity as a place that no longer kept him stuck but which instead fueled his purpose, inspiring the impact he had on many people's lives. It became a place where he found success in life and in his work.

The Impact of Mentorship

Through Land and Chad, I learned the profound impact of being both a mentor and a mentee in different seasons of life. It all began when Land felt a prompt, a nudge he couldn't ignore, to reach out to me after reading about my accident. That single act led to a phone call, a cup of coffee, and ultimately, years of pouring his wisdom into my life. He wasn't just a sounding board; he came alongside me in life, business, and family and helped me tackle the tough questions and see things from new perspectives.

Then, as life would have it, Land asked me to pour into his son, Chad. And so I did. I started meeting with Chad, and through our conversations, what began as mentorship blossomed into a genuine friendship. Chad became more than a mentee; he became a source of encouragement, nudging me to step out of my comfort zone and try things I would've never considered, like public speaking outside of my corporate job. He saw strengths in me I hadn't seen in myself.

Over time, Land and I found our relationship shifting too. It was no longer strictly mentor and mentee. We'd become partners in growth, sometimes swapping roles depending on the day. Despite our twenty-year age difference, I was now able to encourage him, offer perspective, and provide guidance in areas where he needed support. Land would say we are equals now, and our connection is a beautiful exchange where we swap roles as mentor and mentee with ease. It's not about hierarchy; it's about sharing life and the lessons that come with it.

Looking at the three of us, I like to think of it as a triangle—a dynamic support system with each of us pouring into one another—holding each other accountable, offering motivation, and giving perspective. And as a result of this, I'm now a professional speaker and performance coach—a path I might never have taken if it hadn't been for that tragic accident, Land's note, and Chad's encouragement to step onto a stage. They showed me that by embracing my story and sharing it, I could offer hope and guidance to others.

Something I learned in professional speaking school, that I've now said to many others, is this: "You are expertly positioned to help your past self." Let that sink in. Each of us has gone through our own share of trials, challenges, and moments of pain or doubt. We all carry the experiences, insights, and processes that helped us move forward. Somewhere out there is a person who's going through the very struggles you've already navigated. You are expertly positioned to help them.

You have a gift inside of you. It's wrapped up like a Christmas present under the tree. Beautiful wrapping paper. A gorgeous bow perfectly tied. The question becomes, Will you unwrap that gift? Will you share your personal and professional experiences, how you persevered and overcame, and what process or steps you took to push through to be in the position that you're in today? Will you share that gift with others? You see, in my opinion, I believe each of us has that gift, and I would go so far as to say it is our responsibility. It is our duty to share that with others, to share that with the world. It is what you were put on this planet to do. In many ways, it is your purpose.

Take a moment to think about who might be around you—in your circle, your community, your workplace, or even the gym—who needs what you have to offer. Think of that person who could benefit from your story, your insights, and your support. Land saw that in me, and I saw it in Chad, just as Chad went on to support those in recovery who were facing the same battles he once fought. And as I speak, coach, and mentor, I'm paying forward all that's been poured into me.

Mentorship, at its core, is about saying, "I'm here for you. I'll walk alongside you, encourage you, and offer the guidance I wish someone had given me." So who is pouring into you? Who are you pouring into? These relationships, when given the structure and consistency they deserve, can be life-changing. Embrace the gift inside you, the wisdom you've gained from your own journey. Unwrap it, share it, and watch how it ripples through the lives of others.

Just Around the Corner

Life has a way of keeping us on our toes, throwing us into situations we never saw coming. No matter how carefully we plan, how diligently we build our careers, or how precisely we map out our goals, the reality is some kind of devastating event could be just around the corner. It's not something we like to think about. After all, we're conditioned to focus on achieving, moving forward, and "building a life." But if we're not mentally prepared for the unexpected, the things we've built can crumble in an instant, leaving us disoriented and broken.

The question is: how do we face a future that may hold both great promise and potential hardship? How do we build toward success without letting the fear of the unknown paralyze us?

Here's where resilience comes into play. There's a saying that goes, "The only way to get experience is to get experience," and it's the same with resilience. As much as we might want to avoid it, the only way to build resilience is by facing difficulties head-on. You have to go through adversity to understand your ability to survive it. So when life hands you a trial—whether minor or major—the question becomes, do you let it box you in, hold you back, or break you down? Or do you choose to take control of that energy and redirect it toward something positive?

Once you've faced hardship and emerged stronger, you gain a powerful asset: confidence in your own resilience. Even if your experience was with a smaller setback, the knowledge that you made it through can be life-changing. You start to understand that no matter what comes your way, you can adapt, grow, and move forward. And while you don't know when the next big challenge might come, you can expect it without living in fear.

The key is to find a balance between staying grounded in the present and being prepared for the inevitable curveballs life will throw. If you choose a growth mindset and rise to the challenge, taking action, and practicing resilience, you'll develop what I call a "game-time mentality." You won't be easily shaken. And when adversity strikes, you'll be ready—ready to bounce back faster, to refocus your energy, and to turn hardship into something good.

Building resilience takes work and consistency. It's about mindset first: choosing to be adaptable and strong. Then it's about taking action: surrounding yourself with people who lift you up, joining mastermind groups, immersing yourself in learning and coaching, and building a life that actively prepares you for anything. That way, you're creating a foundation that can withstand almost anything.

Don't live in fear of what could happen, but don't be naive about it either. Expect that challenges will come, even if you don't know what, when, or how intense they'll be. Then, build yourself up so that when those moments arrive, you'll have the strength, resources, and perspective to rise above. Life's unexpected trials don't have to derail your journey—they can become the very things that make you stronger.

LIFE'S UNEXPECTED TRIALS DON'T HAVE TO DERAIL YOUR JOURNEY— THEY CAN BECOME THE VERY THINGS THAT MAKE YOU STRONGER.

The accident happened in March 2012, and though over a decade has passed, its impact is still rooted deeply in my life. Emotionally, I'm in a good place now, but that event has shifted my mindset, my priorities, and countless everyday choices. One of the most significant changes? I don't drink alcohol anymore. That decision was one of many influenced by the accident, which became a moment of reflection for me, a reason to reconsider the role of alcohol in my life.

Back then, I thought, What if I'd had a few drinks before getting in the car that night? Just a couple of beers might have tipped the scales, maybe led to criminal charges, or involved me directly in the bar fight—either as a participant or someone injured by it. It's a chilling thought. So, I let that incident reshape how I approach decisions today. I've stopped drinking, I avoid bars, I don't stay out late, and I keep a sharper eye on my driving habits, speed, and surroundings. I saw firsthand that life can be taken in an instant, and I want to live aligned with values that truly matter to me.

That experience became a catalyst for reflecting on life's big questions. Where do I want to invest my time and energy? Am I living in a way that, if today were my last day, I'd be at peace with my choices? I've become more focused on health, relationships, and purpose-driven work—the things that bring real joy and value without the wastefulness of distractions. This mindset shift has helped me redirect the energy of that traumatic night into positive action in my present, and I hope it encourages you to think about your own experiences and ask how you might channel your painful moments into something meaningful.

Of course, there's a spiritual dimension to this too. While this isn't a faith-based book, I've wrestled with the big questions: Is everything predestined? Did God allow this for a reason? I've wondered whether God caused it, allowed it, or what purpose there could be in one man's life being taken, another being put on trial, and me being caught in the middle of it all. But here's the thing—I don't have all the answers to these questions, and I may never find them.

I've come to believe that while we all experience adversity, pain, and loss in different forms, what ultimately matters is how we respond. The power of mindset—making a conscious choice to move forward—has been the key for me. I've found that purpose and healing often come through serving others who may be experiencing something similar. By stepping outside my own pain and focusing on helping others, I find perspective, relief, and a renewed sense of purpose.

So here's my encouragement to you: consider the aspects of your life that might need realignment or reprioritization. Don't just coast through life. Let your challenges become a force that propels you forward. Use your experiences, however painful, as a powerful motivator to create a life of intention, resilience, and impact.

HEALTH, WEALTH, AND SELF

AT THE TIME of this writing, I have been alcohol-free for six years. The last drink I had was at a Wednesday night work dinner, and it was an event that completely changed the way I saw myself and my life.

Work dinners are a familiar scene to many of us in the business world. They begin with a happy hour drink to loosen everyone up, followed by a cocktail (or two) once you sit down for the meal. That particular night, I had one happy hour drink and two margaritas. Nothing over the top. Nothing that would make anyone raise an eyebrow. But it was enough.

The next morning, I woke up groggy and irritable. I fully intended to hit the hotel gym before starting my workday, but thanks to a restless night of sleep brought on by the alcohol, I skipped it. So now I had missed my workout, the one thing that grounds me and sets the tone for my day. By the time I showed up for my work meetings,

I was operating at about 50 percent of my capacity. Half focused. Half effective.

And it didn't end there. After a long day of subpar performance, I climbed into my car for a four-hour drive home. When I finally pulled into my driveway, my wife and my daughter were waiting for me on the front porch. I'd been away for a few days on a work trip, and they were excited to see me. But I was tired and irritable. I looked at them, and I thought, They deserve so much more than this.

To make matters worse, my wife was pregnant with our second daughter at the time. That moment hit me like a punch to the gut: I missed my workout. I gave my employer and clients half of what they deserved. I showed up for my family—my biggest priority—utterly depleted. And I've got another daughter on the way. Don't they all deserve the best version of me?

I had told myself many times before that I was sick and tired of feeling sick and tired. But for whatever reason, that day was different. That day, I said, Enough, and I meant it.

I didn't know then that I would stay alcohol-free for the next six years. I didn't even know if I could make it a week. But one day turned into a week. A week turned into a month. A month turned into a year. And here I am.

That night and the days that followed forced me to confront a deeper question. How had I even gotten to that point? Why did I feel obligated to drink at every work dinner and social event? Why had I allowed something that started with my first sip, maybe at a birthday or a wedding, to turn into a habit that dictated my ability to show up in my life?

It's so easy for small decisions to snowball. The first drink becomes the second. The second becomes five. Then you're drinking at birthdays, weddings, beach trips, work functions. Before you know it, you're having drinks on a random Tuesday night by yourself or ordering a Bloody Mary after church at brunch.

You were fine before you ever took that first drink. You were having fun and living a productive life without it. It took over slowly, one small bad decision at a time. Then, one day, you wake up and realize you're sick of it. You feel stuck and depleted. The cons outweigh the pros, and you know you have to change.

That's where I landed. I realized alcohol had become a barrier to everything I cared about—my health, my work, and, most importantly, my family. So I made a change.

You Deserve a Better You

Back when I was still drinking, my friend Mark shared a story with me that hit home as a father. Mark's teenage daughter, Sarah, was at a sleepover with some friends one Saturday night. Later that evening, Sarah called Mark and said, "Dad, there's some drama here with the other girls. I don't want to stay. Can you come pick me up?"

Mark paused. He'd been drinking at home, and he couldn't safely drive to get her. "I'm sorry, sweetheart," he said. "I can't come get you. I've had too much to drink. But I'll send Mom."

Sarah insisted, "No, Dad. I want you to come get me."

Mark couldn't. He wasn't doing anything "wrong," technically. He was drinking at home like so many people do. But because of that choice, he couldn't be there for his daughter when she needed him most. He told me how much it tore him up. And as he spoke, I imagined my own daughters—one already born, the other on the way.

I never wanted to be in that position. I never wanted alcohol to be the reason I couldn't show up for my family. I wanted to be someone my daughters could always count on. And I knew that if I wanted to live long enough to watch them grow up and have their own families, I needed to take control. But it wasn't until that work dinner that I finally took that first big step toward a better future.

Alcohol might not be a problem for you. Maybe you're struggling with your health, your finances, your career, or your relationships. No one sets out to be unhealthy, broke, or unfulfilled. It happens through small choices that compound over time until you look up and wonder, How did I get here?

But the good news is you can stop. You can pivot. You can make a different choice. And when you're truly sick and tired of feeling sick and tired, that's when you'll create the urgency to change. Your family, your career, your friends and coworkers, and you deserve nothing less than the best version of yourself.

Take Care of Your Health

I often wonder what life would have been like thousands of years ago. Simpler, I imagine. Back then, survival was our only priority: hunting, gathering, moving with the seasons. There was clarity in that simplicity. Today, it feels like there's a new health fad every week: vegetarian, vegan, paleo, Atkins, carnivore, high-carb, low-carb, high-fat, low-fat—the list goes on. You could get lost in calorie counting, macronutrients, and micronutrients if you're not careful. While each diet has its merits, I believe the real power lies in mastering the basics: whole foods, fresh fruits and vegetables, lean organic meats, water over soda or juice, and nutrient-dense nuts, berries, and seeds.

Or start even simpler, with whole foods, unprocessed ingredients, and no added sugars or alcohol. Forget the constant calorie scrutiny for a moment. If you simply eat whole, natural foods, you will feel and be healthier. Caloric balance matters, yes, but mastering the basics offers immediate benefits that are undeniable.

The same goes for fitness. Whether you love basketball, tennis, weightlifting, cycling, or group classes, it doesn't matter as long as you stick with something. Pick your activity, or even a mix of activities, and commit to them three, five, seven days a week. Show up consistently, week after week, and the results will follow. People often get hung up on selecting the "perfect" program, but success usually lies in the habit, not in finding the ultimate workout.

Over the years, I've observed that people often sacrifice their health for corporate success, chasing titles and wealth, sometimes at the cost of their own well-being. Picture the top salesperson, awarded for their exceptional performance, yet battling high blood pressure, overweight by fifty or even a hundred pounds. Are they fully aware of the toll this pursuit takes on their health? Will they regret trading their well-being for career success if it means facing a shortened life? It's a question that stays with me. Why not prioritize health from the start?

SUCCESS USUALLY LIES IN THE HABIT.

Imagine if you could simply eat better, move more, and find fulfillment in community and exercise. Not only would it enhance your quality of life, but it would make you show up better in your relationships, at work, and as a parent. Most of us want to see our kids grow up, to become grandparents, to retire with our health intact so we can travel and enjoy life on our terms.

So, why not control the controllables—focus on health, master the basics, keep it simple, stay consistent, achieve results? Those small, steady steps compound over time and lead to a life that's not only longer but also richer and more fulfilling. Commit to a healthier version of yourself and don't sacrifice that part of you for the relentless demands of today. Because here's the truth: ten years from now, you don't want to be looking back with regret, wishing you'd prioritized your health before it was too late.

Now, when I speak about health, I often get questions from people in demanding careers—sales professionals, for example, who are constantly stretched thin, racing from meeting to meeting, chasing that next deal or quarterly target. They're climbing a unique kind of corporate ladder built on relentless schedules, client calls, and nonstop responsibilities. They'll tell me, "I just don't have the time to prioritize health. I'm trying to close deals, exceed quotas, build relationships. What time can I possibly carve out?"

And it's not just salespeople. Many people, even those working long hours in minimum-wage jobs, face similar challenges. For some, it's about survival. Working sixty to eighty hours a week just to keep food on the table and pay rent doesn't leave much time—or energy—for anything else. The reality is that not everyone has the same opportunities, flexibility, or control over their schedules.

But for those of us with some degree of choice—those in roles where we command a good wage, own a car, have savings and some investments—the question becomes: Is sacrificing your health worth climbing that ladder? If your relentless pursuit of career success is costing you your health, it might be time to reassess. It's a tough pill to swallow, but you might have to take a step back—downshifting, accepting a lower position, changing companies, or even pivoting careers. Yes, that's a big move. But if it means a more balanced, healthier life, isn't it worth considering?

This leads me to a concept I often explore in my talks: the Legacy Statement. Ask yourself, "What do I want to be known for? What do I want to be remembered for? And to whom does that matter most?" When I ask this, most people say it's their family—their spouse, kids, maybe a close friend or two. They don't mention colleagues, bosses, or clients. They say they want to be known as a good partner, a devoted parent, a person who was present, who gave and loved unconditionally.

So here's the next question: If your family is who you want to matter most to, is the way you're living aligned with that? If being there for your family is at the core of your legacy, if you want to watch your kids grow, to be a grandparent one day, to spend as many days as possible with your spouse, then health cannot be a sideline—it must be the foundation. If you're going to be there for the people you love and set a good example to the kids who are looking to you, then you have to make hard choices that allow you to take care of yourself.

This is the moment for you to choose: to focus on what matters most, to say no to the things that ultimately don't serve you, and to start taking the small steps that will allow you to live your legacy, not just chase a title.

Maybe climbing the corporate ladder at a big Wall Street firm, striving for status and position, works for some people. Either they're content with their legacy as it stands, or they haven't paused to make the tough decision to step back for the sake of balance in their health. But very few people truly "have it all." In fact, when I see the most "successful" people on stage, collecting awards, being celebrated, I sometimes find myself feeling sorry for them. Because I know—behind the scenes—they're sacrificing more than people realize. Health is usually one of the first things to go.

The cost of relentless pursuit doesn't stop at health, either. It often spills over into other areas—self-care, relationships, even purpose. And what does it all matter in the end? So many who suffered heart attacks, who lived lives marked by high blood pressure, high cholesterol, or relentless stress, might look back from the other side with regret if given the chance. If they could come back, would they do it all the same way? My guess is probably not.

Why am I saying all this? My goal here is to minimize future regret—especially the kind that could be avoided by tending to your health now. I know people have unique circumstances and challenges. Some face genetic conditions, health issues that make weight management difficult, physical ailments, or metabolic limitations. This isn't about judging anyone or making blanket assessments. My intention isn't to make people feel bad but to shake them awake. It's about asking, "Have you taken a moment to pause, long enough, to truly assess what you're sacrificing?"

So many people get wrapped up in the identity that comes from career success. It feels good to move up the ladder, to gain status and recognition. But have you stopped to consider how much of your health—and possibly your legacy—you're giving up in the process? When you really sit with it, is there a misalignment between how you're living today and how you want to be remembered? And if so, are you ready to pull those future regrets into your present awareness and create a sense of urgency to act?

It starts with recognizing that change doesn't require extreme measures. It's about simplicity and consistency. Health, like any other area of success, is a journey of cumulative habits, not one-off efforts. I want you to reach a point where the need for change feels urgent, a moment where the pain of staying the same outweighs the discomfort of change. Let the fear of future regret drive you. Let it fuel a transformation that you'll look back on with pride.

Make the commitment to your health a burning priority. Keep it simple. Stay consistent. See the results. Let this not be a fleeting, week-long attempt but a lifestyle shift. Let it be a daily choice you're willing to make, knowing that you're investing in a future you who will thank you for taking action today.

Take Care of Your Wealth

Now, let's talk about wealth. A lot of the same principles apply here— keep it simple, stay consistent, achieve results. When people hear the word "wealth," they think of money, stocks, assets, liabilities—essentially, personal finance. But I see wealth in simpler terms. Wealth is about intentional choices that give you control, so you're no longer simply reacting to expenses or hoping there's enough in the bank by month's end.

Early on, I recognized that if I made a thousand dollars, I wanted to decide what would happen with that thousand rather than letting it slip away on expenses. There's a concept called "paying yourself first" that is incredibly powerful. Before covering bills, before spending on anything else, you decide how much of that money you're going to save and invest for your future. Even a modest goal—say, setting aside 5 to 20 percent—can lead to huge results over time. And for those who are really committed, maybe even 30 percent. If you earn a thousand dollars, that would mean putting aside $50 to $300 right away into savings and investments before doing anything else with the money. By paying yourself first, you're building a foundation for future wealth.

Next, before diving into daily expenses, consider how much you want to give away. I'm talking about charitable giving—a commitment to causes you care about, whether it's supporting your local church, a charity, or an organization close to your heart. It could be 5 or 10 percent of your income, but the key is deciding upfront. Let's say that's another $50 to $100 from that thousand you just earned going to something meaningful, perhaps cancer research or a community project. The point is, before any rent or bills are paid, you've already prioritized yourself and the people or causes that matter to you.

So now, what's left over is what you live on. You look at what remains and ask, "How much can I afford for rent? What kind of car fits my budget? How often can I dine out? What type of vacation is realistic?" You've already put yourself first, you've given to causes you care about, and now you can see clearly what's left for everything else. When you approach wealth this way, you set a foundation that, over the years, will grow into something truly significant.

This framework—pay yourself first, give to charity, then spend what's left—is life-changing over the long term. If you adopt it early on, ten, twenty, thirty years down the line, you'll find yourself in a solid place financially, free from the constant stress of debt and overspending.

And with every dollar, you'll be aligned with your purpose, building a legacy that reflects who you are and what you care about.

Of course, there's more to consider as you go along. Life insurance, disability insurance, and estate planning are part of a well-rounded wealth strategy. Having documents like a simple will or trust ensures that if something unexpected happens, you've already determined how your assets will be managed. And if you have children, these plans provide for their future care and designate who will take on guardianship if needed. Preparing for these scenarios is part of simplifying wealth—having plans in place so that no matter what happens, you've taken care of the essentials.

In today's complicated financial world, it's easy to get lost in noise—stock market fluctuations, economic forecasts, political shifts, and the endless advice streaming from social media. But here's my suggestion: simplify. Master the basics. Do those things consistently—week by week, month by month, year by year. When you do, you will set yourself up for the kind of results most people dream about but rarely achieve. Too many get distracted, chase trends, make poorly timed choices, and end up with less than they could have had. But by sticking to a simple, proven approach, you can build real wealth, and, more importantly, a legacy that aligns with your values.

Take a moment to pause, reflect, and think about your next financial steps. The decisions you make today can set the path for a lifetime.

Take Care of Your Self

Finally, you need to take care of "self." I'm using the term "self" as a bit of a catchall. What I'm really talking about is all the facets of life that make up who you are. It covers mindset and beliefs, relationships—whether that's dating, marriage, parenting, friendships, or community.

It includes career decisions, business goals, sales strategies, leadership, and personal growth. It's the whole spectrum of what shapes us.

When was the last time you invested in yourself? I'm not talking about a work training that came with the job. I mean, really investing in yourself, out of your own pocket, to create genuine change. For most people, personal development ends somewhere around high school or college. If they played sports, they had coaches, maybe some support from a training department early on in their career. But as the years go by, how many of us actually think to bring in an extra set of eyes or ears to guide us, to assess where we're at, and to push us to the next level?

In my experience, very few people consider taking money from their bank account and putting it into their own personal growth. Yet that's exactly what can make the biggest difference. When you invest in yourself, you get someone to help you see your blind spots, to provide perspective, to lay out a plan and hold you accountable. Growth isn't about going at it alone. It's about realizing where you could use a coach to motivate, refine, and guide you in becoming a better version of yourself each day.

Think about this: It's impossible to be both the player on the court and the coach watching from the sidelines. When we're in the thick of it, we can't always see what we're missing. That's why I believe so strongly in having "skin in the game." If you're truly committed, you'll invest your time, energy, and yes—your money. With those stakes, you're more likely to see real transformation. It's no longer "messy action." It's intentional, purposeful movement toward your goals. You've got someone to come alongside you, to encourage and keep you accountable to your highest aspirations.

This brings me to a concept I love: the gap and the gain. Credit goes to Dan Sullivan and Dr. Benjamin Hardy here, but the idea is powerful. So many of us get stuck focusing on the gap—the distance between where we are now and where we want to be. We fixate on what's missing, what we're not, and how much further we have to go. But what if we shifted our focus to the gains? However small, every step forward is a win. Day by day, week by week, the gains accumulate, and before long, you're closer to your goals than you ever thought possible.

Are you investing in yourself? What areas of your life or business need improvement? How well have you done on your own? There's a saying that goes, "If you were going to do it, you would've already done it." So ask yourself: Are you taking action or just thinking about being the change? Maybe you're taking messy action, but without a coach, a plan, and accountability, you're not reaching your potential.

ASK YOURSELF: ARE YOU TAKING ACTION OR JUST THINKING ABOUT BEING THE CHANGE?

Or maybe you're putting in some effort but not quite getting the reps in—the disciplined practice it takes to reach the next level. What you need is a game-time mindset, ready to step up anytime, anywhere, with anyone. Are you prepared to get to the outcome you're after?

Do you have skin in the game? Are you truly invested in yourself? Where are you stuck, and how can you close that gap? Start focusing on the gains—the small victories that build momentum. It's about controlling what you can, showing up consistently, and remembering that every intentional step you take is bringing you closer to the life you want. Taking care of "self" is about more than just success—it's about growth, purpose, and legacy.

CONCLUSION

LET'S END THIS journey where we began, with a moment of reflection. Think about areas in your life—personal or professional—where you've faced adversity, pain, setbacks, or challenges that feel unresolved. These struggles might be keeping you stuck, causing frustration, sadness, or anger.

Now, imagine redirecting some of that energy into a force for good, transforming it into something purposeful.

HOW YOU STARTED DOESN'T DICTATE HOW YOU FINISH.

Sometimes, in the very places where we feel the most pain, we can discover the seeds of our purpose, a deeper drive that could guide us toward a positive impact. This shift can lead to profound changes, enhancing your health, enriching your relationships, or even igniting new paths in your career. It may even inspire a business or mission that's rooted in using your adversity as an advantage.

Remember: how you started doesn't dictate how you finish. Life may stack the odds against you, but you get to choose whether you let them weigh you down or use them as fuel for change—not only for yourself but also for the people around you and even for generations to come.

In a world filled with endless social media feeds, artificial intelligence on the rise, political and social divides, global conflict, and widespread loneliness, I encourage you to pause. Just stop long enough to consider a simpler approach. Picture life before cell phones, before the constant internet connection, before streaming services replaced face-to-face interactions. Imagine a time when people walked more, gathered more, connected more. When neighborhoods came together for cookouts, when community and faith groups were vibrant, when we called each other instead of texting and shared stories in person instead of in snapshots. There's power in returning to the basics, in focusing on simplicity, consistency, and meaningful results across all areas of life—your health, your wealth, your self-improvement, and ultimately, your satisfaction.

So here's my shake-up, wake-up call. It's an invitation for you to stop, reflect, and recalibrate your life toward what matters most. What do you want to be known for? Who does it matter most to? Take an honest look at your Legacy Statement—the core of who you want to be and the impact you want to make—and then identify where there might be a disconnect between that vision and how you're actually living.

I invite you to try a simple exercise. First, ask yourself, "What do I need to stop doing?" What's draining your energy, pulling you out of alignment, or proving to be inefficient and ineffective? Whatever it is, dare to let it go.

Then ask, "What do I want to continue doing?" Identify the things that light you up, the tasks and activities that fall within your zone of genius, the things that feel natural and effortless. Time flies when you're doing these things, and others recognize the positive impact they bring. Commit to continuing these activities wholeheartedly.

Finally, ask, "What do I want to start doing?" Think of new habits, goals, or routines that align with your vision for health, wealth, self-improvement, and personal growth. These are the things that resonate with your Legacy Statement, the things that bring you energy, joy, purpose, and fulfillment. Don't let others' expectations or the pressures of societal standards keep you from honoring what matters to you. Whether it's the corporate ladder, social demands, or title pressures, this is about creating a life that's authentically yours.

So, here's my final statement: You deserve this. You deserve to prioritize yourself, to work through this process, to let go of what doesn't serve you, to double down on what does, and to start fresh with purpose. If you can go through this alone, wonderful. But if you need

"WHAT DO I NEED TO STOP DOING?"

"WHAT DO I WANT TO CONTINUE DOING?"

"WHAT DO I WANT TO START DOING?"

guidance, reach out to others who can support you, whether that's a friend, a mentor, or a coach. Don't wait. You have a choice to make your life meaningful, to build a legacy that truly reflects who you are and what you stand for. Don't wait another day!

ABOUT THE AUTHOR

LANCE CIBIK IS a keynote speaker and performance coach who defies the odds. Despite facing overwhelming challenges from the start, he has transformed adversity into purpose, impact, and success in both life and business.

Raised in a paycheck-to-paycheck environment, Lance lost his mother to suicide at just one year old and was living independently by age seventeen. A tragic car accident in his early thirties further tested him when he accidentally took a man's life. These experiences, however, sharpened his focus and resilience, fueling his commitment to simplicity, consistency, and achievement in all areas of life and business.

Despite his circumstances, Lance became a first-generation college graduate and built over two decades of success in sales and leadership within the financial services industry. Today, he inspires thousands through his impactful keynotes and coaching services. He graduated from the University of North Carolina at Charlotte with a degree in business administration.

Outside of speaking and coaching, Lance can often be found on the basketball court, contributing to his community through volunteer work, or spending quality time with his family.

www.ingramcontent.com/pod-product-compliance
Lightning Source LLC
Chambersburg PA
CBHW031441120626
46545CB00006B/2507